cocktails, snacks & amazing
nonalcoholic drinks
from the heart of hollywood

Clarkson Potter/Publishers
New York

TREJO'S Cantina

DANNY TREJO

with HUGH GARVEY

Published in the United States by Clarkson
Potter/Publishers, an imprint of Random
House, a division of Penguin Random House
LLC, New York. ClarksonPotter.com

CLARKSON POTTER is a trademark and
POTTER with colophon is a registered
trademark of Penguin Random House LLC.

Library of Congress Cataloging-in-
Publication Data is available.

ISBN 978-0-593-23548-5
Ebook ISBN 978-0-593-23549-2

Printed in China

Photographer: Ed Anderson
Food Stylist: Lillian Kang
Food Stylist Assistant: Paige Arnett
Food Stylist (LA/cover): Veronica Laramie
Editor: Raquel Pelzel
Editorial Assistant: Bianca Cruz
Designer: Jen Wang
Production Editor: Mark McCauslin
Production Manager: Kelli Tokos
Compositors: Merri Ann Morrell,
Nick Patton, and Hannah Hunt
Copy Editor: Kate Slate
Indexer: Elizabeth T. Parson
Marketer: Stephanie Davis
Publicist: Kristin Casemore

10 9 8 7 6 5 4 3 2 1

First Edition

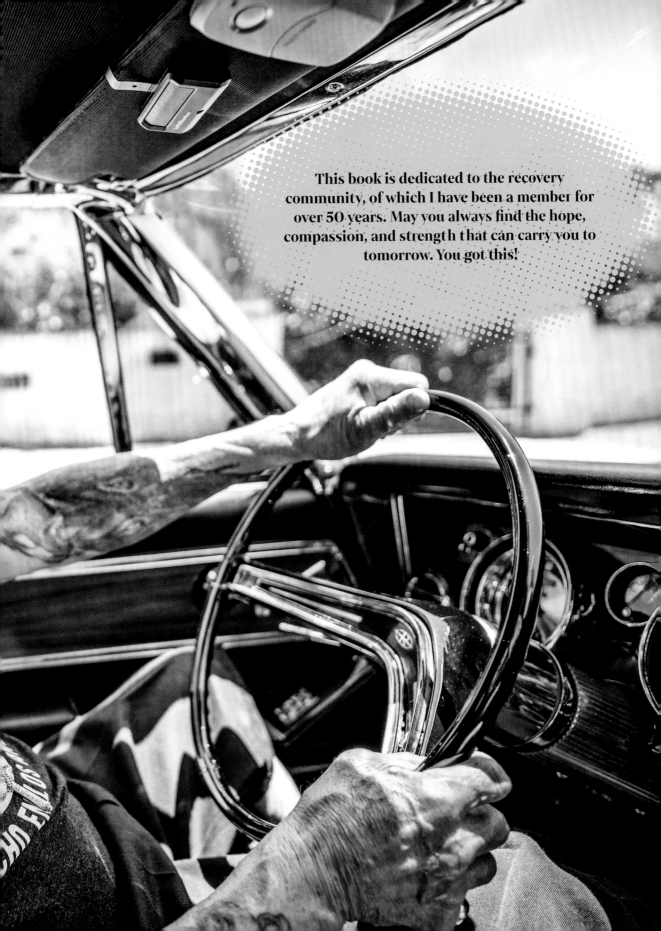

This book is dedicated to the recovery community, of which I have been a member for over 50 years. May you always find the hope, compassion, and strength that can carry you to tomorrow. You got this!

Contents

Hola
FROM HOLLYWOOD

The technical definition of a cantina is a Mexican restaurant that serves drinks. But culturally, cantinas are a lot more than that. When I was growing up in Los Angeles, they were places on the side streets of downtown or the East side where men would gather to get away from the heat of a hot summer day, the challenges of life, hang with their friends, have a drink, and feel like they belonged. You could say they're in my blood since I've been hanging out in them ever since I was a kid.

One of my earliest childhood memories is tagging along with my dad and uncles to the oldest Mexican settlement in LA and where, after church on a Sunday, we'd sneak into the cool dark of one of the local bars. This was due east of Hollywood some ten miles, on Olvera Street. They'd have their drinks (I'd have a soda) and there'd be a spread of snacks; nothing fancy, just cheese and sandwiches laid out for the guys. I think it was their way of getting guys to stay at the bar and not leave to go eat

somewhere else. So it makes sense that I opened my own cantina smack-dab in the middle of Hollywood, my favorite neighborhood in the city I call home.

The irony of all of this—that I would open a watering hole known for food and drinks—is not lost on me. I haven't touched a drop of alcohol in over fifty years. But for me, it's not about the cocktails or alcohol per se but about the point of a cantina: They're festive gathering places where people come to enjoy life and celebrate one another's company. I opened mine to be all inclusive to nondrinkers and drinkers alike—and we have fun drinks and cocktails as well as food for vegans, vegetarians, and people doing gluten-free and paleo—as well as for meat-and-potato guys, like me. We've all got our paths, and no matter what they are you gotta eat and you gotta eat well. And that's what this book is all about: easy food that's a celebration in every bite.

Hollywood is a neighborhood I'd cruise to back in the '60s when I was running around causing the kind of trouble that got me locked up in San Quentin. One wrong move and my life could've ended in Hollywood, but by the grace of God I became a working actor instead. Now Hollywood is home to my Trejo's restaurant empire. Going from movie "bad guy" to restaurateur is a Hollywood second act that I've been enjoying almost as much as acting.

In my first cookbook, *Trejo's Tacos,* I shared the food that taquerías are famous for: sometimes healthy, slightly modern twists on classics, like my mom's barbacoa brisket, our award-winning cauliflower tacos, our killer breakfast burrito, and donuts that come in the brightly colored box with my mug on it (it proves real men do wear pink!). It taught you how to cook the Trejo way in the comfort of your home.

In this book I'm going to share more of the kind of Mexican food that Angelenos like me eat every day. Which is to say fun and easy food with big bold flavors. There are taquitos you can riff on, tostadas you can swap toppings on, and spicy Mexican Thousand Island dressing you'll be slathering on every damn sandwich. Empanadas you can make meaty or vegan, birria tacos just as good as the ones you get at Tijuana-inspired taco trucks all over the city, the bacon-wrapped jalapeño-spiked hot dogs called Danger Dogs sizzled on hot-rodded shopping carts outside Dodger Stadium on late nights, and even the fight-night nachos I serve my friends when we're hanging out at my house in

the San Fernando Valley. There's a chorizo burger inspired by the holy burger trinity of LA: In-N-Out, Bob's Big Boy, and Fatburgers. And in the spirit of something for everyone, we've also got some damned fine vegetarian tamales that are so delicious you'd swear they were made with manteca!

And since this is a book about recreating Trejo-style cantina vibes at home, we've got drinks that are a celebration of this great city and of life itself. Hollywood is home to historic bars where bartenders have been slinging cocktails in saloons and restaurants like the Brown Derby, Musso & Frank Grill, the Cock 'n Bull, and Tiki-Ti long before mixology became a trend. We've taken many of the classic cocktails served at these spots and updated them with a Mexican twist.

But like me, not everybody drinks alcohol, so it was important to me to have drinks that were just as delicious and sophisticated and celebratory as our cocktails but that didn't have alcohol. To make the cut, they needed to stand on their own and make you say: "Damn this is good!" Just don't call them mocktails. If I'm throwing a party, everyone gets a seat at the table.

A quick rewind to 2020, when I started working on this book: The party was going hard at the cantina, and then the world turned upside down. First, the pandemic ravaged our city, killing thousands and forcing people to hole up in their homes, terrified. Soon after, the killing of George Floyd and the protests that followed hit us hard—there was marching in the streets and out-and-out combat with the police. The Trejo group of restaurants shut down for the first time in their history. No tacos were slung on La Brea. Our taco truck was parked for good. The cantina, closed. The farmers' market, usually bustling at all hours, was a ghost town like the rest of Los Angeles. Some of the world ground to a halt, but not me. I'd rather look for a solution than be a part of the problem.

Ever since I got out of prison, I've sought to comfort people rather than seek comfort, and

Covid didn't stop me. I hit the streets with my consigliere, Mario, another ex-con with a heart of gold. We helped the homeless by handing out food and thermal underwear. It's what I've been doing for decades and, if anything, we ramped up the outreach during the pandemic. As soon as we could, we fired up the burners again at the cantina and cooked food for restaurant workers who'd lost their jobs and for the protesters marching in the streets. And yes, for the cops, too. We'd offer food to the cops and they were shocked, like, this is for us, too? Absolutely! We're all doing our best. Even though the restaurants were shut, we kept folks employed and kept people fed to the best of our ability.

Fast-forward to today: Hollywood is open again and the cantina is bustling. And I can't get enough of the neighborhood. It's got the history, the hustle, and the dreams of this great city of LA that I've always called home. It's where to this day I cruise in one of my lowriders on the same streets where I took long midnight walks with my mentor and best friend Eddie Bunker when I was figuring out life. It's the neighborhood that employed me from the beginning: where I helped build the Cinerama Dome, and where the old movie studios and sound stages first put me to work. And it's also where we have our top-secret development kitchen where we act like mad scientists and invent dishes and drinks for the restaurants and our cookbooks, including the one you've got in your hands. Yeah, life was hard for me at points, but I always find the positive no matter what happens, and that's the soul of a cantina: a place to celebrate life with all its complicated surprises and twists and turns. I specialize in twists and turns: thug as a kid, ex-thug sober guy, thug on screen, ex-thug who hugs. And that's what this book is: a big badass Trejo hug. Now go get into your kitchen, cook up something spicy, and join me in celebrating life in all its badass beauty.

The Secrets of CANTINA

COOKING

Think LIKE A PRISONER, *Cook* LIKE A CATERER

When I was in prison, I learned you can make a lot out of a little. Take tattoos, for example. Even though we didn't have any professional equipment, it didn't stop the masters from making some of the most beautiful tattoos I've ever seen.

We'd help them make tattoo needles out of melted-down chess pieces, guitar strings, and toothbrushes. We'd mix up ink from the ashes of burned newspaper in varying shades. And in the end they'd create real art for us. The same ingenuity and community applies to food, too. In my opinion, food is always best when shared. Meals can be a comfort when you or others need it the most. On Sundays at San Quentin, we'd have what we called "spreads" in the yard for the guys who didn't have anyone coming to see them during visiting hours. We'd put together a picnic of snacks and cookies and instant noodles and other things we'd bought at the commissary or hustled from the guards. We'd do what we needed to make it

special: We'd upgrade the noodles with bacon left over from breakfast. We'd tear open a bag of chips and spike 'em with Pico Pica hot sauce. Someone would sneak in some pruno (homemade prison hooch) that he brewed up in his cell. It was a prison potluck. If a bunch of cons can make a concrete table in a maximum-security penitentiary feel like a party, imagine what you can do in your kitchen if you treat every meal—whether it's breakfast, lunch, or dinner—like a celebration of life. When I think back, it's kind of like we turned that little corner of the yard into our version of a cantina.

First and foremost: Cantina food is fun food. Imagine: tasty nibbles you can make a ton of and put out for people to snack on while watching the

game or hanging out with the kids at a pool party, or to even eat as a light lunch throughout the week. We're not talking about preparations you need a culinary degree to perfect. The recipes are easy and forgiving and once you cook it you can make it your own like any good abuela. Just like no two guacamole recipes are the same because everybody has different preferences, I fully expect you to add more salt or less lime or quadruple the jalapeños depending on your taste.

While the last cookbook was primarily recipes from our menu, these recipes are inspired by Mexican classics like tostadas, taquitos, and guisados. They are the foundational elements of Los Angeles Mexican culinary culture.

The recipes in this book are modular—I'm not a fan of rules, and I don't think food should have hard-and-fast ones either. While you'll find recipes for tostadas and taquitos and empanadas, you'll also see fillings and toppings you can swap in and out for one another if you feel like it. Our empanadas are stuffed with beef and pickles, but you can put that filling on a tostada if you feel like it. Chicken tinga goes in tacos here, but you can load it into taquitos if you want. This is why I like to say that at Trejo's, we think like a prisoner—with ingenuity and gratitude—but cook like caterers, which is to say, with practicality in mind.

THE CANTINA PANTRY

At Trejo's, we've mastered the art of cooking for crowds. We know what will "hold"—meaning taste good the minute it's made but also hours later when the guests show up—like braised meats and blended salsas whose flavors actually meld over time. We know which ingredients to rely on when you need to move fast (canned black beans are amazing) and how to smartly dress them up so they taste like you've simmered them for hours (add a slice of bacon and chile de árbol to deepen the flavor). Here's what we have on hand to pull off cantina food fast, what you should add to your pantry, and why it works.

The Holy Trinity: Cilantro, Onion, and Lime

Every line cook in a Mexican restaurant has cilantro, onion, and lime at their station. And if you're going to be cooking from this book, these three ingredients are nonnegotiable. No matter what the season or the dish, there is virtually no food (okay, maybe our watermelon paletas!) that can't be improved by this combo. The Trejo's Cantina chefs call these ingredients "aromatics," which makes sense when you think about it. They all smell good in their own way and add a nice fragrance (and flavor) to your food. Take my basic avocado and tortilla snack. Do like I do and slice up an avocado (I pick one from the tree outside my home), put it on a warm corn tortilla, add your "aromatics," and you're on your way to a pretty fantastic meal.

You'll see them on condiment tables or applied to tacos *con todo* ("with everything") at every taco stand and food truck in LA. because they're nonnegotiable. It would be like peanut butter without jelly!

ONIONS: Onions are pungent and sweet and add crunch. They also balance out the richer flavors and creamy textures of Mexican food. White onion is the most common kind used in Mexican cooking, but hey, yellow and red work, too. Rules are made to be broken, right? And if you don't have onion on hand, swap in scallions or shallots.

CILANTRO: This herb is all about freshness and bright bite. It's tender like parsley, basil, and oregano—meaning it should always be added at the end of cooking, and not the beginning. Some people hate cilantro, though, and think it tastes like soap. That's a mild reaction you can't get around, so leave it out if you need to. If you're looking for a decent sub, fresh marjoram and oregano aren't traditional, but they bring on flavor and freshness, as does parsley. While you need to pluck marjoram and oregano leaves off their woody stems, the fact is the tender upper part of the stems of cilantro (and parsley) are not only tender, but have a ton of flavor. The real art is in the rinsing and drying. Nobody wants a gritty or soggy garnish. The order of business with cilantro is this: Cut the bushy leafy top off the bunch, tender stems and all, and put it in a colander. Rinse it under running water and let it drain, then wrap it up in a kitchen towel to absorb excess water. Place it on a cutting board and chop it until it's like confetti.

LIMES: Zippy and tangy flavors play an important role in Mexican dishes, which is why so many are finished with a squeeze of lime—from the filling of a taco, to a slice of ripe mango, or as the tart garnish of a tequila cocktail. Citrus also resets the palate in between bites of rich food—the acidity kind of wakes your mouth up! If you can find the little round Mexican or Key limes, that's great—they're

floral and sprightly and sweet. But standard Persian limes (the kind you usually find in the grocery store) are what we use at Trejo's because they're so readily available. No matter what variety of lime you use, they ain't cheap, so you want to maximize the precious juice you extract. The trick is to roll the lime on the counter with your palm to soften the membranes, slice it in half crosswise, place the halves in a hinged citrus squeezer and press the juice through a wire-mesh sieve into a bowl. Voilà: seed-free fresh juice!

Holy Canned Trinity: Chiles, Beans, Tomatoes

CANNED CHIPOTLE PEPPERS IN ADOBO SAUCE:

This is the flavor cheat of the century. Smoky, spicy tangy, sweet, and deeply flavored canned chipotles—marinated in tomato sauce, vinegar, salt, and spices—add punch and mystery to marinades, sauces, salsas, and creams, and show up over and over in this book. They're pretty spicy and a little goes a long way, so you should use these sparingly. If you want all the flavor with less heat, scrape out the seeds. You're probably never going to use an entire can in one dish, so be sure to transfer the extras to a glass jar, cover, and refrigerate. They keep for about 1 month.

Riffs: Mix chipotles with sour cream for an easy taco topping. Stir into maple syrup to amp up your pancakes. Spike your vinaigrette for spicy salad. You can chop them finely and add to poultry, beef, or chicken marinades. Use the adobo sauce in soups, or leave the chipotles whole in braises.

CANNED BLACK BEANS: Cheap and cheerful, when served with rice, these building blocks become a complete protein. (Once a bodybuilder, always a bodybuilder!) Sauté some onion in a skillet, add a bay leaf, dried chile de árbol or a sliced jalapeño, toss in those beans with some water, and you're cooking like a grandma.

Riffs: Smash cooked beans with a fork and spread on a tostada, serve with rice and top with shredded cheese, cilantro, and onion and you've got the cheapest, tastiest complete protein on the planet. Puree and thin with chicken broth and top with the onion, cilantro, and a squeeze of lime for a simple soup.

CANNED TOMATOES: I'm not letting the Italians take all the credit: Mexicans know how to make the most of canned tomatoes, whether it's canned tomato sauce or canned peeled tomatoes. You can use either to enrich rice, use as a base for salsa, and simmer with onions and chiles to braise meats.

Riffs: When you're cooking rice, start by sautéing onions, then mix in ¼ cup of tomato sauce after you've sautéed the onions to make it "Spanish." Blitz a can of peeled tomatoes in a blender along with half an onion, a couple garlic cloves, a jalapeño, cilantro, salt, and lime for fast salsa!

JARRED OR CANNED PICKLED JALAPEÑOS: Tangy heat resets every rich bite of food. Pickled jalapeños should be in your fridge at all times! Scatter over just about any dish in this book. You can buy whole ones and chop them yourself, or buy the presliced rounds.

Riffs: Chop and mix into mayo for a spicy burger spread or French fry dip. Chop and add to cilantro and onion for a 1-minute Mexican pickled relish.

The Spice Rack

ANCHO CHILE POWDER: With just a little heat and warming sweetness, this is a kinder, gentler alternative to cayenne and can go in sauces, marinades, on poultry, meat, and fish.

GROUND CUMIN: Earthy and mysterious, like me! Kidding aside, this is like the bass player in a band. It lays down the low end on which all other flavors riff. Use in sauces, rubs, and marinades.

DRIED OREGANO: If you can get Mexican oregano, go for it. It's a little more pungent, woodsy, and sweet than the Mediterranean version, but that kind works just fine, too.

CHIPOTLE CHILE POWDER: Not quite the magic bullet of its canned counterpart, ground dried chipotles are still a great way to get dusky smoke flavors into a dish without sparking up a wood-fired grill.

TAJÍN: This brand of Mexican chile-lime seasoning is tangy and spicy—it's the classic street cart fruit topping. Add flavor to the rim of a glass for a cocktail or nonalcoholic drink, sprinkle on whipped cream with your pancakes, or use it to dust sautéed chicken breast.

HOT SAUCE: Obviously! In the prison commissary, we'd get Pico Pica taco sauce and put it on just about everything. You can't go wrong with Tapatío and Cholula.

All Things Masa

Masa is the foundational starch in the cantina pantry. Cornmeal that's been "nixtamalized" (the word comes from the Aztecs, the O.G. badasses of Mexico) with lime (not the citrus, but calcium hydroxide) to make it more digestible and tender. The Italians use durum wheat to make pasta with hundreds of different regional shapes, and Mexicans use masa to turn into tortillas, sopes, huaraches, gorditas, tlayudas, tamales, and more!

Tortillas

When I was growing up, everybody made tortillas from scratch. Back then if you bought tortillas, you were kind of looked down on. We'd wrap everything in a tortilla, even hot dogs. The first time someone gave me a hot dog with relish and onions on a bun I was confused. I was like "What is all this bread?"

MASS-PRODUCED TORTILLAS: Commercially produced supermarket tortillas made with instant masa work in a pinch, and you'll often find them doubled up to use for tacos at stands. This is because they're thin and fall apart when soggy (think of juicy tinga filling!), so stacking two keeps the whole thing together.

ARTISANAL CORN TORTILLAS: Thicker and made with real fresh masa, these are sturdier and more filling than the standard stuff. More expensive but worth the cost because they're loaded with deep, sweet corn flavor. Plus you don't need to double them up. Mexican markets sometimes sell fresh masa. If you can track down masa made from rare heirloom Oaxacan corn, that's even better. The Oaxacans are the masa masters!

Masa Harina

MASECA: The most widely available brand of instant masa. Made from fresh masa that's been dehydrated and powdered. Use to make home-made tortillas, but don't expect them to be as tender or tasty as the stuff handmade at restaurants and made from fresh masa.

ORGANIC MASA HARINA: Baking big-shot brand King Arthur has gotten into the masa game and makes some really fine organic masa that you can buy at the supermarket. The flavor is fuller and a little earthier than Maseca.

HEIRLOOM MASA HARINA: There's a new crop of companies importing bags of ground masa made from Oaxacan heirloom corn varietals, and they're changing the game on what folks can do at home. Order online and you're tapped into some real centuries-old traditions and supporting small-scale Mexican farms, too. Look for the brand Masienda.

The Tortilla Press

Whether made from wood or metal, a tortilla press helps crank out tons of tortillas for a party that are always of even thickness (or thinness). The heavier the better—you want the press to do the work for you.

Classic Mexican Cheeses

I'm not shy about my love of Monterey Jack cheese even though it's not technically Mexican (or maybe it is? It was made by Franciscan monks in the Monterey peninsula in the early days of California shortly after it became a US state). Here are some other favorites that you'll find in cantinas everywhere—as well as in these recipes.

COTIJA: Salty, crumbly, and to some folks a little stinky, this is a great finishing cheese to sprinkle on soups, elotes, and salad. It's sort of the Parmesan of Mexico.

QUESO QUESADILLA: A semisoft white cheese that melts beautifully and, you guessed it, is perfect in quesadillas.

ASADERO: Stringy and mild, this white mozzarella–like cheese is originally from Oaxaca.

THREE-CHEESE BLEND: You'll see this the most throughout the book. It's my favorite blend of cheese—Monterey Jack for that tangy flavor, mild asadero so it melts easily, and queso quesadilla for more mild meltness. I love it in burritos, tamales, and more, thanks to its balance of flavors and textures.

QUESO FRESCO: Soft, super mild, and tangy-sweet, this velvety cheese is unaged and a milder alternative to Cotija. Sprinkle it on top of black beans or enchiladas.

QUESILLO: Super stringy and briny, this Oaxacan cheese is the traditional topping for the pizza–like Oaxacan street snack tlayuda.

Mexology
HOW TO BUILD A CANTINA-STYLE HOME BAR

My dad built his own bar at home, and because of it I got to meet Clint Eastwood. That's right, when I was ten years old Clint Eastwood actually drank a beer in my living room. This was long before Eastwood became a legend thanks to Sergio Leone's iconic Spaghetti Westerns and *High Plains Drifter*, not to mention *Dirty Harry*. Back in those days, Eastwood was a relatively unknown actor until he landed the role of Rowdy, a hotheaded cowboy on the popular TV show *Rawhide*.

My dad worked construction for a real estate development company and between gigs he'd manage their apartments. The *Rawhide* cast was living in the building my dad was managing on Vineland and Riverside in the San Fernando Valley. He also just happened to have finished building this little bar in our home's living room. He saw Eastwood and the guys in the elevator and was so proud of his newly minted bar, that he had the cojones to invite them over!

This was decades before I knew being a movie star or action hero was a viable career. All I remember is walking into the living room and seeing a bunch of pretty cool guys drinking beers with my dad. There was one guy who stood out—I couldn't stop looking at him. He had a power you couldn't miss that made you think this guy is going to become either a serial killer or president. Thank God he didn't become either one. He's now one of my all-time-favorite movie star heroes. Even though, if we were cast in the same film, we'd probably end up on either side of a movie gunfight!

Bartending is a craft that's been practiced at the highest level in Hollywood since the golden era. To serve others a drink is a privilege and not only an extension of hospitality, but of connection—like, share a minute with me, let's get a drink. Even though I don't drink, I still frequent restaurants with bars when I'm working or taking meetings. I'm a regular at one of Hollywood's oldest and greatest homes of the martini: Musso & Frank Grill, which has been open since 1919. You might've seen it in any number of movies and most recently in my buddy Quentin Tarantino's *Once Upon a Time in Hollywood.* It's got all the things you expect in an old-school saloon: dark wood booths with Naugahyde benches, waiters in red tuxedo jackets and bow ties, soaring ceilings painted with murals and stained with tobacco smoke. They're known for their great steaks and ice-cold martinis served with a little pitcher of extra martini on the side. They've served any number of Hollywood icons over the years and not just Brad Pitt and Leo DiCaprio: noir detective writer Raymond Chandler drank there and put it in his books, Humphrey Bogart, Rudy Valentino, Keith Richards, you name it. Rumor has it that way back when there was a bookie who would take bets at the counter. Like I said, I don't drink, so I go there for their amazing pot pie. But that's that thing: They do food perfectly, and good food and good drinks go hand in hand, just like at a cantina.

Musso's is just one of the spots in LA and Hollywood known for mixology, the fancy word for bartending. Now you can't seem to go out to dinner at a nice restaurant without coming across a bartender who you swear went to grad school to learn how to make drinks served with herb-infused this and muddled that. In Hollywood, it's not uncommon to be charged upwards of 20 bucks for a drink! When you stop to consider the ingredients, the labor, and the smarts they put into it, it's worth every penny—these are not drinks to be knocked back, but rather meant to be savored—they're the main event.

At Trejo's our bartenders practice what you could call "Mexology." Like our food, it's a mash-up of Mexican influences and LA vibes with a dose of Trejo attitude. While the flavors may lean Mexican, the recipes themselves are based on the foundational techniques and ingredients of craft cocktail making. Just like a chef has a go-to set of pots and pans and a well-stocked pantry to be able to make amazing dishes that make up a good menu, a great bartender has their favorite bottles, syrups, garnishes, and gear to be able to make their drinks at the highest level. Learn the foundations, and you'll know how to make sours, martinis, highballs, rocks drinks, and any of the classics.

If you're like me, however, and don't drink or if you want to offer a nonalcoholic drink at a get-together, skip ahead to Badass Booze-Free Drinks (page 42), where we get into the wonders of non-alcohol drink making. I promise you, drinks made without alcohol can be just as fun and creative as their spirited cousins.

THE THREE MAIN STYLES OF COCKTAILS

Making drinks is easier than you might think. While there are hundreds if not thousands of individual cocktails, there are only three main styles that are the foundation of them all. Kind of like cars, trucks, and motorcycles: You can paint them different colors, swap out engines, and add turbochargers or racing seats, but the chassis is the same.

The Sour

The formula is 2 ounces strong to 1 ounce sweet and 1 ounce sour. That's the ratio for the daiquiri, the Rob Roy, the Greyhound, and the holy grail of Mexican cocktails, the margarita.

In the case of a margarita, you're mixing 2 ounces of tequila to 1 ounce of simple syrup and 1 ounce of lime juice. But swap in white rum for the tequila and you have a daiquiri. Use vodka as the strong and grapefruit as the sour and you have a Greyhound—or use lemon juice instead of grapefruit and you have a Lemon Drop. And so on. Memorize that ratio of 2:1:1 and you've got one-third of the cocktail canon down pat.

You do need to know why it works to make it work. Sours always contain fruit juice, most often some tart citrus, which is why they're called sours. Then, there's sugar to balance the sour. The contrast becomes a dance between hero and villain, good cop and a bad cop, Darth Vader and Luke Skywalker. They each play a slightly different role and one without the other makes for a drink that's a hell of a lot less interesting.

And they need to be integrated with liquor. The way you do that to a sour is by shaking them in a cocktail shaker with ice. That emulsifies the three liquids, which is the fancy term for mixing them up real good. If you want three very different sorts of liquids to get along, you gotta rough 'em up a little with that ice and shaking.

And you've got a couple of choices about what to do with them once you've mixed them together: You can serve them "up," which means without ice, most frequently in a martini-style glass or cocktail coupe. Or you could serve them on the rocks—the rocks being ice, of course. If you serve them on the rocks you don't need to shake them as much since the melting ice in your drink will continue to dilute it as you sip it. (For more, read The Importance of Ice, page 34.)

The Highball

Like the name says, this cocktail is a high—or tall—drink. Typically, a highball is less strong than other kinds of drinks because it has more mixer in it. The combination usually consists of a base spirit with an effervescent mixer like tonic (such as in a gin and tonic, for example), club soda (as in a scotch and soda), or flavored soda (like a rum and cola).

The highball is the easiest drink to make, as it's not as precise in its measurements or technique. These are often called "pop and pours" because all you need to do is pop the top on a soft drink and pour it on a spirit over ice and you're good to go. Some good examples are the Moscow Mule made with vodka and ginger ale and the Paloma made with tequila or mezcal and grapefruit soda.

The Aromatic Cocktail

The martini sits in the category of aromatic drinks like Manhattans and Negronis, which are spirit-forward with no fruit juice and therefore very boozy. At its most basic, this style of drink is typically made from a base spirit and a fortified wine or aperitif like vermouth. There's the martini, which is vodka or gin and dry vermouth. The Manhattan is with bourbon and sweet vermouth. The Negroni is gin and a double whammy of sweet vermouth and a bitter aperitif (most often Campari). The ratio changes here, but it's usually 2 ounces or so of the base spirit plus 1 ounce or so of the modifier.

Regardless of what James Bond said about the martini, he was wrong. The martini and other drinks of its sort should be stirred to gently chill down and dilute some of all that alcohol with water, but not water it down too much. Shaking melts the ice too quickly and while you'll end up with a cold drink, it will be too watery. Just like sours, you can serve these "up" in a martini or coupe, or on the rocks.

THE SPIRITS

If you go to a supermarket or liquor store it can be overwhelming to see the hundreds of spirits brands, but the reality is just like with the three main cocktail formulas (see page 27) that unlock hundreds of variations, it's the same with spirits: There are only a handful you need. I advise you to stick with what you like and not be bothered with brands other people are into. Luckily most of the cocktails in this book use tequila or mezcal as a spirit. The others call for the base spirits that are the foundation of all the classic cocktails, like gin or rum. So you only really need a few varieties to set you on your way to cantina cocktailing.

Tequila

The granddaddy of Mexican spirits. Made from the blue agave, this spirit long ago overcame its reputation for being low-quality stuff with a worm in the bottom. That bad reputation came from mass-produced cheap tequila that spring breakers in Tijuana overindulged in, which unfortunately tarnished the reputation of the entire category. The fact is that there are dozens of brands that make excellent versions of tequila in the traditional way: Farmers take mature agave plants (those spiky-looking things that folks think are cactuses but are in fact a plant related to the crocus) and chop off the spiky leaves, leaving the heart of the agave, called the piña, intact. The piña is then roasted and distilled, producing that clear pure spirit that's an expression of the plant and land.

Mezcal

A close cousin to tequila, this spirit is also made from agave. In recent years mezcal has gained in popularity due to its wonderfully smoky flavor. While tequila is primarily made in the state of Jalisco and only from blue agave, mezcal is grown throughout Mexico, in states like Oaxaca, Guerrero, Puebla, and many more, and can be made from over a dozen different types of agave.

Like tequila, mezcal can be aged to various degrees, so you'll find joven, which is similar to blanco, as well as reposado and añejo styles (see Types of Tequila, opposite).

The vast majority of mezcals you'll find on the market are made from the Espadín variety of agave (it's the easiest and fastest to grow), however mezcal made from other more rare varieties are worth searching out; look for varieties like Tobalá, which is sweeter and fruitier, and Cuishe, which is more herbal and minerally.

Gin

Made with any number of botanicals, herbs, and spices like juniper, ginger, star anise, and more, this originally British and Dutch spirit shares a lot of ingredients with the Mexican pantry, like coriander, allspice, and cinnamon. It's bright, sharp, aromatic, and bracing.

Bourbon

The quintessential American whiskey. Bourbon can be made anywhere in the country, but its most famous brands are from Tennessee and Kentucky. Distilled mostly from corn, then aged in oak, it's a caramel-sweet and smoky spirit often used in a Manhattan, whiskey sour, or old-fashioned.

Types of TEQUILA

Vodka

The most neutral of spirits. Vodka is a blank slate that gives proof or bite to a drink and can have any flavor thrown at it. Think of it as the chicken breast of the back bar: On its own it doesn't taste like much, but it'll absorb and amplify the flavors you add to it—like espresso for an espresso martini or olive brine for a dirty martini. In these cocktails, vodka is just along for the ride.

Rum

The quintessential tropical spirit made from sugarcane. Originally from the Caribbean, it pairs well with fruit juices and citrus, which is why it's so good in Hemingway's favorite drink, the daiquiri. My business partner Ash Shah starts every vacation with a piña colada—for many, rum is the on-ramp to a party!

Scotch

The national spirit of Scotland. Also referred to simply as whisky (no e), you've got two styles: blended, which is (more) affordable and simpler in flavor, and single malt, for which malted barley is heated over a smoky peat fire, then fermented and aged almost like a vintage wine. They say you can taste the salt of the seaside Scotch and the earth of the highlands. You could say mezcal is the scotch of Mexico.

BLANCO

Unaged and crystal clear, this is the baseline tequila for mixed drinks and most margaritas. Light in color and taste, it gives a Mexican spin to our chile-flavored Ancho Mojito (page 90) and is the foundation of our Lavender Paloma (page 97) and other cocktails.

REPOSADO

Straw-colored, this is tequila that's been lightly aged in wood, most often oak. It has a light caramel sweetness and can be enjoyed on the rocks or mixed. It's the mellow star of our variation on the Old Pal, which we call the Viejo Vato (page 118).

AÑEJO

This is one step up from reposado in intensity of flavor and smoothness and richness due to having spent more time aging in wood. It's best for sipping or saving for super-special cocktails like our mole bitters–spiked spin on the Old-Fashioned (page 122).

GEAR

When I was in prison we used to practice our own sort of mixology, but we didn't use a cocktail shaker: Our main mixology gear was a plastic bag we'd use to make prison hooch, aka pruno. We'd mix up sugar and fruit juice and bread and let it ferment in that bag near the heaters and pay the guards to not "notice" it. While I'm assuming you're not going to make pruno in a plastic bag, I do expect you may want to purchase some bar gear to make mixology fun and easy. That said, you could pull together a home bar using plastic deli containers (the kind used for soup or anything saucy) and use them as shakers. Some folks use mason jars. But if you can swing it, there's nothing like a gleaming set of stainless steel or copper strainers, shakers, and measuring tools to make you look good and make mixology easy on the eyes and your body—whether you're making cocktails with alcohol or not. Luckily, good sturdy professional bar gear isn't that expensive, either.

BOSTON SHAKER: This is the stainless steel shaker that the pros use. Many bartenders pair it with a similarly shaped mixing glass, which gets inverted (after adding spirits, ice, or whatnot to the metal shaker) into the shaker and then slapped in tight to form a vacuum seal. In recent years more folks have been using two metal pieces—the Boston shaker and a metal cocktail tin—to do the same thing: They're lighter and unbreakable. Unlike the cobbler shaker (see below), you need a separate strainer to strain drinks.

HAWTHORNE STRAINER: Flat and fitted with a spring cap that helps keep it from sliding around when used to cover a shaker and pour out the contents, this is the one-size-fits-all strainer that pro bartenders prefer because they can put it on top of a mixing glass or a metal cocktail tin and strain whatever drink they're making. The vertical slits keep it from dripping too much.

COBBLER SHAKER: This is a shaker that has a built-in perforated strainer and little cap that goes on top. They're cool looking on the bar top, but a little cumbersome to use and can make a mess. But if this is what you got, by all means use it.

MUDDLER: This stick looks like the kind of billy club cops used to carry around. It's the perfect tool for smashing fruit, citrus, and herbs in the bottom of a shaker as you do for a mojito.

COCKTAIL SPOON: The slender and long-handled spoon used to mix stirred drinks like Manhattans and martinis. You can also use it to taste the drink before serving it to see if it needs more juice or alcohol. Just like food, you should taste as you mix and adjust the drink to suit your taste (just no double-dipping, por favor).

JAPANESE MIXING GLASS: Also known as a Yarai pitcher, these faceted thick-walled little pitchers are great for making stirred drinks and look like something out of *Mad Men*.

HINGED CITRUS JUICER: Critical for juicing limes for margaritas and lemons for other cocktails.

The JUICES

MESH SIEVES: Sometimes you want all the flavor of a pureed fruit, but not all the pith and fiber. Get yourself a set of mesh sieves in small, medium, and large in both fine and medium-fine gauges. Some pureed fruit is too thick to go through the truly fine gauge. A tea strainer is fine in a pinch, but if you're going to be making a lot of cocktails, get yourself the real deal.

GOOD PITCHER: Some of the nonalcoholic drinks in this book require enough labor that you want to make a large batch so you can enjoy the drink over a few days or serve it at a party. A good pitcher with a handle and pouring spout will be the thing you'll want to use to serve your creation to friends. You might also want to buy some 1-quart deli containers with lids to freeze any leftovers for future use or to give as gifts.

GOOD BLENDER: If you're going to be mastering drink making, you owe it to yourself to get a good workhorse of a blender. My restaurant staff swears by the Vitamix. It's more expensive than most blenders on the market but also has an insanely powerful motor, is built like a tank, has a crazy-long warranty, and can do at least twice the work of other blenders in half the time.

Lemons and limes are the workhorses of the bar. If you read The Sour (page 27), you already know that they're the foundation of sour cocktails. They're great year-round and you should always have a few on hand, because they're a crucial ingredient in so many cocktails and as a garnish for many other drinks. But citrus will oxidize over time, which changes the flavor, so it's best to use fresh juice the day it's squeezed.

As for other fruit, lean into the seasons and use fruit when it's at peak ripeness. So in the summer use fresh strawberries to make the Red Alert (page 55) and in fall pears for a Fall Guy (page 65).

Fresh tropical fruits aren't always readily available in the US, so sometimes you'll have to use canned or boxed mango, pineapple, or guava nectar, which is just fine. Frozen papaya concentrate is incredible, in fact. And they all keep for a long time.

THE IMPORTANCE OF ICE

A lot of folks think ice is just there to make a drink cold, but that's only half the story. The other half is that it's a critical ingredient that melts and combines with the other ingredients and dilutes the strong stuff, mellowing out the harsh edges and emulsifying the drink (a fancy word for thoroughly incorporating ingredients). When James Bond says "shaken not stirred," he's talking about dilution. Think about it: Shaking makes the ice collide and chip pieces off each other, which then melt and dilute the drink faster and make it just a little frothy when you pour it into the glass. Old-school martini purists stir martinis to gently chill them down and slowly expose them to the ice, which ever so gently melts to achieve a smoother effect.

The Ice Rules

Ice Rule 1:
Shake drinks made with fruit juice

Fruit juice is a heavier weight or viscosity than alcohol and needs the agitation to blend it with the booze. Fruity drinks also usually have some thickish simple sugar syrup in them that needs to be incorporated. On top of that, you often have tart lime or lemon that needs the edges rounded off, and a good bash in the shaker will take care of all of that. It's sort of like making salad dressing: You have to whisk it all up to blend it thoroughly. And when you do shake, please shake it like you mean it: which is hard and machine-gun fast for 10 seconds (count slowly, shake quickly!), strain, and serve immediately. The legendary turn-of-the-century bartender Harry Craddock said you should drink a cocktail when it's still laughing at you.

Ice Rule 2:
Always stir "aromatic" drinks

Drinks made with fortified wines like vermouth and Campari and other spirits but no fruit juice should be stirred. The thinking here is they're very precisely calibrated ingredients that people like monks fussed over for centuries to get the flavors, spices, and infusions just right, so they need a more delicate hand to get along—you don't want to spoil the balance by diluting them with ice.

Ice Rule 3:
Always Use Fresh, Solid Ice

Ice in a bag from the gas station or supermarket is good for cooling down sodas or beers in a tub but is *not* meant for cocktails! Those cubes have holes in them and will melt *super* fast, leaving you with a watery, warm drink. No thanks. Instead, use solid pieces of ice—even ice from your refrigerator's ice machine is better than bagged ice! So plan ahead and make a few batches of ice cubes if you're going to be making cocktails for a crowd. You can also invest in those silicone ice cube trays that make perfect cubes and spheres.

Also *please* make sure your ice is fresh! If ice has been sitting in your freezer for more than a week or so, chances are it's taken on the smell of your frozen pizzas and leftovers. If you drink filtered water, use it (or bottled water) to make your cubes—if your tap water has off-tastes like chlorine, you don't want ice made from it in your perfectly crafted drink.

GLASS— WARE

You could serve a cocktail out of a jam jar if you felt like it (or a red Solo cup if that's more your speed), but, if you are interested in classic barware, there are a few shapes that are nice to have on hand.

ROCKS OR LOWBALL
The short squat glass you serve strong cocktails over ice in.

COLLINS GLASS
This is basically a tall glass like you'd serve water in—also called a highball glass. Use it for tall drinks served with soda or other effervescent liquids like gin and tonics, Palomas, and Moscow Mules.

MARTINI OR COCKTAIL GLASS
The smaller the better, as in 8 ounces or less. The cocktails in this book are designed to be small and will never fill those big resort-size glasses that fit two to three servings in one glass. Cocktails are for tasting, not chugging! You could also get a little narrow and tulip-shaped Nick & Nora glass named after Nick and Nora Charles, the heroes in the famous noir detective novel and classic movie *The Thin Man*. You can also get a cocktail coupe, the inverted dome-shaped glass also used for champagne, but nice for any "up" drink.

The Secrets
OF THE
BOOZE-FREE BAR

*AND THE PRINCIPLES OF
MAKING AMAZING ALCOHOL-FREE
DRINKS AT HOME*

When I stopped drinking alcohol some fifty-plus years ago, I started drinking a lot of stuff that wasn't necessarily all that great for me. Sugary drinks were pretty much the only alternative if you didn't want to drink club soda, water, or coffee. In the penitentiary, I'd drink Pepsi, Coke, Kool-Aid, or iced tea. After I got out, my go-to drink at a party or bar would be cranberry and Sprite. When I didn't want that much sugar I'd go for a cranberry and soda. Not a thrilling menu of options.

What a difference it is for nondrinkers today. We are living in the golden era of nonalcoholic drinks and it's hands down the best time in history to be sober. Not only are bartenders experimenting with booze-free drinks that have all the inventiveness and creativity of mixology, but there's a whole range of zero-alcohol wines and "spirits" that are infused with herbs and spices and have backbone and bite without relying on ethyl alcohol. There are even a number of bars opening up that don't stock a single bottle of booze. They've got the bar and the bar stools, the sound system and the cool, fun people—and they stay open late—but they don't have the alcohol. While some folks like to call a drink without alcohol a mocktail, I don't think that word does justice to these new delicious creations. They're not "mock" anything. They're totally original, authentically delicious, and true to themselves. And they'll never give you a hangover or a DUI!

Because you're not going to be relying on spirits for flavor, you're going to need to learn a few basic preparations, tools, and techniques to make the nonalcoholic drinks in this book. You're going to be using fresh juices for natural sweetness, body, and flavor; fresh herbs for aroma; spice-infused syrups for additional depth; and sometimes even tea for tannin (that raspy bite that makes your tongue a bit dry).

Making these drinks is actually a lot more like cooking than mixing liquids as you might for a margarita or old-fashioned. And just like cooking, you can modify things to suit your own taste. Is something too sweet? Then cut back on the sugar. Is a spicy syrup not spicy enough for you? Then by all means double up on the chiles. And once you learn the principles of zero-alcohol drink making you'll be improvising your own nonalcoholic drinks at home in no time.

LEARN THE SECRET FORMULA

(THAT ISN'T REALLY A FORMULA)

While there's no strict ratio of components that makes a successful nonalcoholic cocktail, there are some loose guidelines—and in a word they all add up to "balance." Typically there are three primary components: a base flavor, a modifier that complements the base flavor, and a flourish that ties it all together. The base ingredient is what gives the drink its primary flavor, and most often it's a fruit. The modifier can be a syrup or a tea infused with spices that go with the base flavor. And then flourish can be a fresh garnish or final touch of extra spice or extra acid that makes everything sing. You want a little sweet, a little tangy acid, and a lot of deliciousness.

Here are a few tips to help guide you on your quest for preparing perfect nonalcoholic cocktails:

Use Fresh Juices Whenever Possible

These drinks are special, so make a point of using the best in-season produce possible. The flavor will be fullest, the natural sugars at their peak, and your drink that much more amazing. However, some fruits are hard to get, which is why I think it's okay to use canned pineapple juice and guava nectar when needed (unless you're lucky enough to live in the tropics!).

Learn the Language of Agua Frescas

Like the name suggests, agua fresca is a refreshing water-based drink that gets extra flavor from fresh fruit juice, a little sugar, and sometimes seeds or grains. If you've ever been to a Mexican restaurant in LA, you've probably seen the watermelon, hibiscus, and horchatas lined up in big dispensers or oversize jars with ladles. Adding water to a base of fresh fruit juice is an economical way of scaling up a big batch of drinks while preserving some of the fresh fruit flavor.

Make Infused Syrups

Simple syrup is what bartenders use to add body and sweetness to drinks. Typically equal parts sugar and water, they're also a great way to add extra flavor to a drink when you infuse the syrup with spices, herbs, or chiles. All you need to do is combine sugar and water with your flavorings (dried chiles, peppercorns, woody herbs, whatever!) in a pot, bring it all to a boil, and then take it off the heat and let it cool down. The flavors of the ingredients in the syrup will transfer into the syrup and voilà! You've got yourself an infusion. For a more truly Mexican spin, try infusing agave syrup (yes, made from the agave plant) the same way.

LOS
ANGELES
MON
AMOUR

Try Infused Teas

If you've ever brewed a cup of tea you're already an expert on making infused teas. Just do the same thing—boil, steep, let cool—but with dried edible flowers like hibiscus, spices, ginger root, or any other aromatic ingredient added to the pot. A "tea" doesn't have to have tea leaves—it can be herbal, too, as in mint, chamomile, or lavender.

Add Acid

I've said it before and I'll say it again: A little fresh lime juice goes a long way. Acid in fresh citrus is a great way of turning "on" a drink. A lot of fruit already has a ton of acid (think strawberries, some tangy apple varieties, grapefruit), but when a drink is pretty good but could be better it often needs just a little bit more acid and that's where your friend the lime (or lemon) can help.

Yes, Salt

This is actually a pretty truly secret ingredient that bartenders use more than you'd think. While you've seen salted rims on margaritas, adding a pinch of salt to a drink can deepen its flavor and balance it even more. Salt suppresses bitterness on the tongue so adding it can actually ironically make a drink taste sweeter!

Badass
BOOZE-

I like Shirley Temple the actor a lot more than Shirley Temple the drink. And these nonalcoholic drinks developed in our Top Secret Hollywood culinary laboratory behind triple-locked doors (kidding) are some of the most delicious things I've ever tasted and prove that you don't need booze to make a grown-ass sophisticated drink that tastes like a full-on celebration. Loaded with enchanting spices, seasonal tropical fruits, and balanced with infusions, these drinks will blow your mind. And you won't have a hangover the next day!

Whether you're sober, sober curious, or drinking less for physical, mental, or spiritual health reasons, I feel pretty confident that you'll find something here that speaks to you. Some are wholly original multistep project drinks you can make in big batches to sip throughout the week or share with your family and friends. Others are single servings you can whip up to toast the day, while some are based on Mexican classic cocktails. As with any recipe I've ever shared, I encourage you to take or leave what you want, and modify to your liking. Some people like more lime, others like it spicy, while others have a sweet tooth. Only you know what you like, so treat each recipe like an expert suggestion or starting point but not a strict set of rules. By now you might've picked up that I'm not a big fan of rules, but I do like delicious things. And now that I have these drinks around I will never have to drink a Shirley Temple again! Cheers to that!

Manzana Verde

You the Mango

Red Alert

Manzana Verde

Apples are one of my favorite snacks, so when I first tasted this apple-based agua fresca, inspired by the Mexican soda Manzanita Sol, I thought it was so delicious that I shouted "We should bottle and sell this!" And then I tried the next nonalcoholic drink and shouted: "We should bottle and sell this!" And I kept saying that about nearly every drink in this chapter. But I still love this one the most because it taught me how fantastic nonalcoholic drinks can be. This one is tangy, crisp, just a little sweet, and the cinnamon—a big spice in Mexican cooking—always tastes good with apples.

5 medium green apples

2¼ ounces (¼ cup plus ½ tablespoon) fresh lime juice

6 tablespoons sugar

3 ounces (¼ cup plus 2 tablespoons) Cinnamon-Honey Syrup (recipe follows)

Salt

12 ounces (1½ cups) club soda

Ice

Core and quarter 4 of the apples and place in a blender. Add 16 ounces (2 cups) water, the lime juice, and sugar. Blend on high until the mixture is completely smooth. Strain the liquid through a large fine-mesh sieve into a 2-quart pitcher. Add the cinnamon-honey syrup and stir. Add salt to taste. Shortly before serving, halve the remaining apple and cut into ¼-inch-thick slices for garnish. Just before serving (so that the bubbles stay lively), top with the club soda, and gently stir to combine. Pour the mixture into six tall ice-filled glasses and garnish with the apple slices.

recipe continues

CINNAMON-HONEY SYRUP

MAKES ABOUT 2½ CUPS

Honey, apples, and cinnamon are a classic flavor trio. Use the leftover syrup anywhere you need sweetener: in hot or iced tea, on oatmeal, or drizzled over toast and peanut butter.

2 cinnamon sticks

1½ cups honey

In a dry small skillet, toast the cinnamon sticks over medium heat for 2 to 3 minutes, until warm and fragrant. In a small pot, bring 8 ounces (1 cup) water to a boil. Once the water is boiling, remove from the heat and add the cinnamon. Let steep for 15 to 20 minutes. Add the honey and stir until it's completely dissolved. Once cool, strain and store in the refrigerator.

Cantina Hack

OTHER DELICIOUS WAYS TO USE LEFTOVER SIMPLE SYRUP

When you make a batch of flavored simple syrup, don't just use it for drinks. Try it:

* **As a substitute for simple syrup in classic cocktails to add a layer of spice**

* **To sweeten morning coffee**

* **When baking granola**

* **Tossed with fruit salads**

* **Instead of maple syrup or honey in cakes and cookies**

* **On pancakes or waffles**

Trejopache

Makes about
TEN 6-OUNCE SERVINGS

Inspired by the fermented Mexican pineapple drink tepache, this tangy spiced drink is custom made for fans of pineapple. Chamomile grows all over California and is a big part of Mexican cuisine—it also goes really well with fruit. Adding Mexican baking spices makes this a really complex and satisfying drink. Piloncillo is raw and unrefined sugar and is naturally brown and deeper tasting than regular sugar and mellower than brown sugar (which is just white sugar that has molasses added to it). You can find piloncillo in the Latin American food section at some grocery stores and online.

1 cup piloncillo (or brown sugar or palm sugar)

1 pineapple

10 whole cloves

2 cinnamon sticks

2 tablespoons dried chamomile

Juice of ½ lime

2½ tablespoons granulated sugar

Ice

In a large pot, bring 2 quarts (8 cups) water to a simmer over medium heat. Once simmering, remove from the heat and add the piloncillo. Stir until the piloncillo dissolves.

Carefully peel the pineapple, discard the rind, and halve the fruit lengthwise (through the stem). Slice into ¼-inch pieces. Place 10 slices in an airtight container and set aside in the fridge to use as a garnish.

In a large pitcher or bowl, combine the cooled piloncillo liquid, the pineapple, cloves, cinnamon sticks, and chamomile. Using a nonreactive plate or bowl, weight the solids down so that nothing is floating above the top of the liquid. Cover the container with plastic wrap. With a toothpick or paring knife, carefully poke holes into the plastic wrap to allow for some airflow.

Allow the mixture to sit at room temperature for 24 to 36 hours, until the liquid is both tart and sweet. Strain the liquid through a large fine-mesh sieve into a 3-quart pitcher. Mix in the lime juice and granulated sugar until the sugar is dissolved.

Pour into tall ice-filled glasses, garnish with the reserved pineapple slices, and serve.

Grapefruit Expectations

Makes
1 DRINK

The earthy cumin-and-pepper agave syrup added to fresh grapefruit juice makes this refresher extra special—if you keep some syrup on hand, it's easy to whip up this drink at a moment's notice. Just slice up some citrus, squeeze it into a glass, and spike it with the agave syrup for a tangy, tasty, subtly spiced earthy beverage.

1 ounce (2 tablespoons) grapefruit juice

½ ounce (1 tablespoon) fresh lime juice

1 ounce (2 tablespoons) Black Pepper–Cumin Agave Syrup (recipe follows)

Ice

A grapefruit wedge, for garnish

In a rocks glass, stir together the grapefruit juice, lime juice, agave syrup, and 3 ounces (6 tablespoons) water (also really great with club soda). Add ice, garnish with the grapefruit wedge, and serve.

BLACK PEPPER–CUMIN AGAVE SYRUP

MAKES ¾ CUP

1½ tablespoons whole black peppercorns

¾ teaspoon ground cumin

¾ cup agave syrup

In a small dry skillet, toast the peppercorns over medium heat until warm and fragrant, 2 to 3 minutes. Remove from the heat and set aside.

In a small saucepan, bring 2 ounces (¼ cup) water to a boil. Remove from the heat and add the peppercorns and cumin. Let the mixture steep for 15 to 20 minutes. Add the agave syrup and stir until it's completely dissolved. Once cool, strain and store in an airtight container in the refrigerator for up to 10 days.

Morchata

The classic Mexican comfort drink horchata is typically made with rice, cinnamon, and some sort of creamy milk. This version calls for dried fruit and tasty pumpkin seeds giving it more flavor and more body, making it even *more* of a horchata . . . or, as I like to say, a morchata!

2 cinnamon sticks

1 cup cooked or uncooked white rice

¼ cup pumpkin seeds

⅓ cup dried cherries

8 ounces (1 cup) whole milk or unsweetened nondairy milk

¼ cup sugar

Salt

16 pumpkin seeds and 8 dried cherries, for garnish

In a small dry skillet, toast the cinnamon sticks over medium heat until warm and fragrant, 2 to 3 minutes. In a medium bowl, combine the cinnamon sticks, 26 ounces (3¼ cups) water, the rice, pumpkin seeds, and dried cherries. Cover the bowl with plastic wrap and allow it to sit in the refrigerator overnight.

Remove the cinnamon sticks and pour the remaining mixture into a blender. Blend until the mixture is smooth. Strain it through a large fine-mesh sieve into a 2-quart pitcher.

Add the milk and sugar and stir until the sugar is dissolved. Add salt to taste. Pour into ice-filled glasses and garnish each glass with 4 pumpkin seeds and 2 dried cherries.

Coconut–Piña–Guava Fresca

Makes
1 DRINK

Yes, you can . . . use canned juices. Tropical fruit juices and nectars are widely available and deliver major flavor no matter what time of year it is. Guava and coconut are best friends, and Tabasco heats up the relationship.

¼ ounce
(½ tablespoon)
fresh lime juice

½ ounce
(1 tablespoon)
pineapple juice

½ ounce
(1 tablespoon)
coconut milk

½ ounce
(1 tablespoon)
Simple Syrup
(recipe follows)

1½ ounces
(3 tablespoons)
guava nectar

1 ounce
(2 tablespoons)
water

Dash of Tabasco

Ice

Lime slice,
for garnish

In a rocks glass, stir together the lime juice, pineapple juice, coconut milk, simple syrup, guava nectar, water, and Tabasco. Add ice, garnish with a lime slice, and serve.

SIMPLE SYRUP

MAKES 1½ CUPS

The brilliance of making a simple syrup is that you can use it for a week and it will inspire. Making your own simple syrup is like making your own chicken stock.

1 cup sugar

In a small saucepan, bring 8 ounces (1 cup) water to a boil. Remove from the heat and stir in the sugar until it dissolves. Transfer the syrup to a clean bottle or airtight container and store in the refrigerator until ready to use.

Red Alert

Makes
FOUR 8-OUNCE SERVINGS

This strawberry drink is made even more delicious by the crazy pyrotechnical addition of charred red bell pepper. Just slap 'em on a grill or straight on the burner of your stove and they'll char and get smoky sweet. Grab a paper towel and clean all that ash off (okay, not "all" but "most" will do). It's like making salsa: You don't have to roast it, but when you do it's so much better. The ancho syrup enhances the smoky and brings the sweet. You're going to love this.

1 red bell pepper

2 cups strawberries (about 16 ounces), hulled

1½ ounces (3 tablespoons) fresh lime juice

½ cup Ancho Simple Syrup (recipe follows)

Ice

Sliced strawberries, for garnish

Roast the red pepper by placing it directly on a hot grill, on a stove's gas burner, or under a broiler. Use a pair of tongs to turn the pepper until all sides are completely blackened. Put the charred pepper into a bowl and cover tightly with plastic wrap. The skin will loosen as the pepper steams. Once the pepper has cooled, remove the blackened skin. Slice the pepper to open it and remove and discard the stem, seeds, and membranes.

In a blender, combine the roasted pepper, strawberries, 16 ounces (2 cups) water, the lime juice, and ancho simple syrup and blend until smooth, 30 to 45 seconds.

Strain the juice through a fine-mesh sieve into a large container or pitcher (discard any solids). Cover and refrigerate the juice until ready for use.

To serve, give the mixture a gentle stir, pour into ice-filled rocks glasses, and garnish each with a strawberry slice.

ANCHO SIMPLE SYRUP

MAKES 3 CUPS

¼ teaspoon ancho chile powder

2 cups sugar

In a medium pot, bring 16 ounces (2 cups) water to a boil. Remove from the heat, add the ancho powder, and let steep for 10 minutes. Add the sugar and stir until it dissolves. Transfer the syrup to a clean bottle or airtight container and store in the refrigerator until ready to use.

Killer Kiwi Agua Fresca

Makes
FOUR 6-OUNCE SERVINGS

Vivid green thanks to the combination of kiwi and Jarritos lime soda, this agua fresca is slightly spicy and sweet and sour in the very best way.

5 kiwis, peeled

2 teaspoons chopped fresh mint

¾ ounce (3½ teaspoons) fresh lime juice

⅛ teaspoon cayenne pepper

Salt

Ice

1 (12.5-ounce) bottle Jarritos lime soda

Kiwi slices and mint sprigs, for garnish

In a blender, combine the kiwis, 6 ounces (¾ cup) water, the mint, lime juice, and cayenne and blend until smooth. Strain the liquid through a fine-mesh sieve into a container (discard any solids). Taste and add a pinch of salt if needed. The mixture should be a bit sour and a little spicy. Cover and store in the fridge until chilled and ready to serve.

To serve, pour 2 ounces of the kiwi blend in an ice-filled Collins glass and top with 4 ounces of lime soda. Garnish with a kiwi slice and mint sprig.

ON EATING, LIVING,
and Staying
IN FIGHTING SHAPE

I've been taking my shirt off for work ever since I played a boxer opposite Eric Roberts in *Runaway Train* back in 1985 and have probably been bare-chested in upwards of 400 movies and TV shows. As far as I know, I'm the only shirtless 78-year-old on permanent display in Madame Tussauds wax museum in Hollywood (see pages 1 and 142). I've got a reputation to uphold! Truth be told, there's nothing like staring at a life-size image of yourself looking pretty lean for a guy who qualifies for membership in AARP to motivate you to continue to eat right and exercise. That said, for me staying fit is not all about my physique: I used to work out for my body, now I work out just as much for my mind.

People always say moderation is the key to health and that's the same with me. "Healthy food" and "exercise" are not separate things but just a part of my life. And I don't mean once a day but throughout the day. The way I build in healthy food and fitness is to put it all right in front of me. Eat what you want but you better stock up on the healthy stuff. I load my fridge with vegetables instead of junk food. That's half the battle: Put health right in front of you and make it accessible. If you're looking at a freezer full of ice cream, then when you're hungry, guess what you're going to eat? If you're looking at a bunch of frozen fruit, though, you're going to make a smoothie instead. I'm always stocked up on apples, red bell peppers, celery, and cauliflower. If I need an avocado I'll just pick one from the tree in my backyard. But it can't be all fiber and no flavor. Just like at the Trejo's restaurants, where we mix vegan, vegetarian, and gluten-free alongside all the classics on our menus, I always make sure to have flavorful foods like ham, turkey, blue cheese, and peanut butter on hand in my kitchen at home. I'll get a celery stick and put peanut butter on it so I get fiber, fat, and flavor all at once. That's the balance.

When I go out to eat in restaurants, it's not about denial. I don't believe in "cheating." I eat whatever I want as long as I don't eat too much of it—I use restraint. Like, why am I going to order a sixteen-ounce steak when I can order an eight-ounce steak and feel perfectly satisfied? Believe me, I could eat all eight of them ribs on a platter, but instead I'll have a few and bring the rest to my dogs (I believe doggie bags should really be for dogs!). They're happy. I'm healthy.

You have to make exercise easy. Everybody asks me, "Danny, how do you stay so fit? I ain't got time to exercise." And I tell them: "You ain't got time to walk? Walk around your damn block! Just walk, that's what I do." Instead of walking all my dogs at once, I'll walk just one of the dogs. I'll come back, get another dog, and walk that one. When I walk by the weight bench I'll do some chest. The next day I'll do it again. It's just part of my routine.

Because I can still run, I've stayed at 170 pounds for about 15 years, a good weight for me. If you make exercise this big rigorous separate thing, it's going to feel like a burden. Instead, I try to bundle a workout with another activity, like doing a quick run on the treadmill before getting on a Zoom. I'll do weights, then I water the lawn. Like they say: Just do it. It's about the mentality. If you say "I have to," you make it into a chore. I'm 78 years old and I don't want another job!

Tamarind Agua Fresca

Makes
FOUR 8-OUNCE SERVINGS

Tamarind is underappreciated in much of the USA. It's a huge part of the Mexican drinks tradition: You'll find it at the agua fresca bars of taco joints, and bottled in sodas across LA. It's earthy and sour and so good, especially when sweetened a little bit, which is what we've done along with adding cinnamon and star anise for holiday spice vibes. You can find tamarind pods in your local grocery in the Latin American foods section.

1 cup dried tamarind pods

4½ ounces (½ cup plus 1 tablespoon) fresh lime juice

8 ounces (1 cup) Spiced Syrup (recipe follows)

Salt

Ice

Cinnamon sticks or star anise pods, for garnish

Remove the hard outer shells of the dried tamarind pods. Place the tamarind pulp and seeds in a medium pot and add 32 ounces (4 cups) water. Bring to a simmer over medium heat. As soon as the liquid starts to simmer, remove the pot from the heat and let it cool for 15 minutes.

Once cooled, use your hands to mash the tamarind pulp in the cooking liquid, separating the pulp from the seeds. Discard all the seeds.

In a blender, combine the tamarind cooking liquid, tamarind pulp, lime juice, and spiced syrup and blend until smooth. Strain the liquid through a fine-mesh sieve into a 2-quart pitcher or airtight container. Add a pinch of salt, stir, and taste. Cover and store in the refrigerator until ready to use.

Pour into ice-filled tall glasses and garnish each with a cinnamon stick, or a star anise, or one of each.

SPICED SYRUP

MAKES 2 CUPS

This is pure holiday vibes in a drink.

1 (¼-inch-thick) slice fresh ginger
1 cinnamon stick
5 allspice berries
2 cups sugar

In a medium pot, combine 16 ounces (2 cups) water and the ginger. Using a muddler, gently crush the ginger enough to break it up a bit. Bring the water to a boil.

Meanwhile, in a small dry skillet, toast the cinnamon and allspice until fragrant and warm, 2 to 3 minutes.

Add the toasted spices to the boiling water and ginger and boil for about 5 minutes. Remove from the heat and let it steep for 15 minutes.

Add the sugar and stir until it has dissolved.

Strain the syrup through a fine-mesh sieve into a large bottle or airtight container and store in the fridge until ready to use.

All Day Baby

This is a low and slow recipe that takes some time to make, but the reward is worth the wait. Simply stated: You make a tea, strain it, add raspberries that will release flavors overnight, and you get a beautiful red drink that's greater in sum than its individual parts. Dried hibiscus, aka jamaica, is in the holy trinity of LA agua frescas (along with tamarind and watermelon)—use it like you'd use any herbal tea like chamomile or mint. The slightly sour note of hibiscus is a nice contrast against the sweetness of the raspberry. Make this in advance for a family get-together and serve it as a welcome drink when they arrive.

**1 cup dried
hibiscus flowers**

⅓ cup sugar

**½ teaspoon
vanilla extract**

6 ounces raspberries

Ice

In a medium pot, bring 32 ounces (4 cups) water to a boil. Add the hibiscus, remove the pot from the heat, and let it steep for 15 minutes.

Add the sugar and vanilla to the hibiscus liquid. Stir until the sugar is completely dissolved.

Strain the liquid through a fine-mesh sieve into a medium bowl or large jug and set aside to cool, about 20 minutes.

Once the liquid is cool, add the raspberries, cover the container, and refrigerate overnight (12 to 24 hours).

To serve, pour into ice-filled Collins glasses and garnish with a few of the infused raspberries.

You the Mango

This is mango salsa in a glass in the very best way. Trust me. And don't skip making the chipotle syrup—it will blow your mind. One taste and you will be drizzling, spiking, and sipping this syrup for days. I love it paired with creamy-sweet mango. You could say it's a study in how opposites do indeed attract.

Tajín, for rimming the glass

Lime or orange wedge

¼ ounce (½ tablespoon) fresh lime juice

¼ ounce (½ tablespoon) fresh orange juice

1½ ounces (3 tablespoons) mango nectar

½ ounce (1 tablespoon) Chipotle Syrup (recipe follows)

Ice

Sprinkle some Tajín onto a small plate. Rub the rim of a double rocks glass with a lime or orange wedge to moisten the rim of the glass. Turning the glass as you go, gently press the wet rim of the glass into the dry Tajín so that it sticks to the glass.

Add the lime juice, orange juice, mango nectar, chipotle syrup, and 1 ounce (2 tablespoons) water to the glass and stir to mix. Add a few ice cubes, gently stir, and serve.

CHIPOTLE SYRUP

MAKES ABOUT 2 CUPS

This smoky-sweet slightly spicy syrup might just become your forever replacement for honey—or sugar, for that matter. Mix a teaspoon and half with soda and lime in a tall glass filled with ice for an instant refreshing DIY spicy lime soda.

1 dried chipotle chile, sliced

2 cups sugar

In a medium pot, bring 16 ounces (2 cups) water to a boil. Add the chipotle and take the pot off the heat. Let the mixture steep for 5 minutes. Add the sugar and mix until it's dissolved. Let the syrup cool.

Strain the syrup through a small fine-mesh sieve into a medium container and refrigerate until ready to use.

The Fall Guy

Just like food, drinks can be seasonal and this agua fresca is amazing in the fall, when pears are ripe, juicy-sweet, and their very best.

2 Bartlett pears,
quartered and
cored

¾ ounce
(4 teaspoons)
fresh lime juice

2 ounces (¼ cup)
Morita and Spice
Syrup (recipe
follows)

Salt

Ice

Pear slices,
for garnish

In a blender, combine the pears, 16 ounces (2 cups) water, the lime juice, and spice syrup and blend until smooth.

Strain the liquid through a large fine-mesh sieve into a 1-quart container. Use a spoon to press the solids into the sieve and squeeze out any remaining juice (discard the solids).

Add a pinch of salt and taste for balance.

To serve, pour into ice-filled rocks glasses and garnish with a slice of pear.

MORITA AND SPICE SYRUP

MAKES ABOUT 1½ CUPS

Not to be confused with Pat Morita from The Karate Kid, *morita chiles are smoked dried red jalapeños. Unlike chipotles, which are also dried smoked jalapeños, moritas are fully ripened before being smoked so they have a sweeter fruitiness.*

1 cinnamon stick

1 star anise

3 allspice berries

¾ cup granulated sugar

½ cup packed
light brown sugar

1 dried morita chile, sliced

In a small dry skillet, toast the cinnamon, star anise, and allspice berries over medium heat until warm and fragrant, 2 to 3 minutes.

In a small saucepan, combine 8 ounces (1 cup) water and both sugars and stir over medium-high heat until the sugar is dissolved.

Add the toasted spices and morita chile and bring to a boil. Remove from the heat and let cool.

Strain through a fine-mesh sieve into a 1-pint container (discard the solids). Cover and refrigerate the syrup until ready to use.

Watermelon Agua Fresca

Makes
FOUR 6-OUNCE SERVINGS

Spicy-tangy Tajín tops off this refreshing drink that reminds me of those street carts you see guys pushing around LA loaded with cubed fruit that you can buy for a couple bucks to cool off on a hot summer day.

2 cups cubed watermelon

2 tablespoons sugar

¾ ounce (1½ tablespoons) fresh lime juice

⅛ teaspoon cayenne pepper

Ice

4 Tajín-dusted watermelon cubes, for garnish

In a blender, combine the watermelon, 8 ounces (1 cup) water, the sugar, lime juice, and cayenne and blend until smooth. Strain the mixture through a fine-mesh sieve into a 1-quart container (discard the pulp).

To serve, pour into ice-filled rocks glasses and garnish each with a cube of Tajín-dusted watermelon.

Mexican-Spiced Cranberry Juice

Makes
FOUR 4-OUNCE SERVINGS

Cranberry juice is one of my all-time favorite beverages. I love how it's sweet but still has that raspy bite. That bite is from tannins, the drying compound that makes tea so good. Here, we infuse cranberry juice with smoky morita chiles and allspice, an underappreciated spice in the Mexican pantry. Allspice is not loud and showy like cinnamon, which makes it a lot like the bass guitar in a band. It's not in your face but it holds everything together.

1 cinnamon stick

4 allspice berries

16 ounces (2 cups) cranberry juice cocktail

1 dried morita chile, sliced

Ice

Lime wedges, for garnish

In a small dry skillet, toast the cinnamon stick and allspice berries over medium heat until warm and fragrant, 2 to 3 minutes.

In a medium pot, combine the cranberry juice, toasted spices, and morita. Bring to a simmer over medium heat, then remove from the heat and let steep for 15 minutes.

Strain the liquid through a small fine-mesh sieve into a medium bottle or container (discard the spices and chile). Store the juice in the fridge until ready to use.

To serve, pour into ice-filled rocks glasses and garnish with lime wedges.

Papaya and Cilantro Agua Fresca

Makes about
SIX 4-OUNCE SERVINGS

Papaya and cilantro are perfect partners. Papaya is so rich and creamy, with a little tropical funk and astringency that stands up to cilantro's fresh peppery bite. Together they make one sweet and refreshingly harmonious drink.

2 cups sliced peeled papaya

1 teaspoon minced fresh cilantro

2 ounces (¼ cup) orange juice

2½ tablespoons sugar

Salt

Ice

Cilantro leaves, for garnish

In a blender, combine the papaya, cilantro, 16 ounces (2 cups) water, the orange juice, and sugar and blend until the mixture is smooth.

Strain the liquid through a large fine-mesh sieve into a 1-quart container (discard the solids).

Add a pinch of salt and taste for balance. Cover and refrigerate until ready to serve.

To serve, pour into ice-filled wineglasses and garnish with cilantro leaves.

Cucumber–Jalapeño Aqua Fresca

Makes
FOUR 6-OUNCE SERVINGS

There are few foods more refreshing than a cool, crisp cucumber sprinkled with salt. Add spicy jalapeño and you have fire and ice! They both have that bright green color and fresh flavors and work really well together. It's sorta like when you put on a great leather jacket. A second ago, you were a regular person, and now you're a badass.

1 medium cucumber, sliced

1 (¼-inch) slice jalapeño

1 ounce (2 tablespoons) fresh lime juice

4 teaspoons sugar

Salt

Ice

16 ounces (2 cups) club soda

Lime slices or cucumber strips, for garnish (optional)

In a blender, combine the cucumber, jalapeño, 8 ounces (1 cup) water, the lime juice, and sugar and blend until the mixture is smooth.

Strain the juice through a medium fine-mesh sieve into a 1-pint container (discard the solids).

Add a pinch of salt, taste for balance, and add a bit more if necessary. Cover and refrigerate until ready to serve.

To serve, pour 2 ounces (¼ cup) of the juice mix into each ice-filled Collins glass. Add 4 ounces (½ cup) club soda to each glass and gently stir to incorporate. Garnish with lime slices or cucumber strips, if desired, and serve.

Carrot and Chile de Árbol Agua Fresca

Makes
FOUR 4-OUNCE SERVINGS

Just because carrots are a vegetable doesn't mean you can't make an agua fresca out of them. Carrot juice is so easy to make and so tasty. I'm convinced if people knew how easy it was, they'd do it more often. Orange juice adds more sweetness and tang, and the árbol chile is a nice hit of spice in the otherwise cooling carrot juice.

2 medium carrots, peeled and sliced into 1-inch pieces

1 dried chile de árbol, seeded and sliced

4 ounces (½ cup) fresh orange juice

2 teaspoons sugar

⅓ ounce (2 teaspoons) fresh lime juice

Salt

Carrot slices, for garnish

In a blender, combine the carrots, 12 ounces (1½ cups) water, the chile, orange juice, sugar, and lime juice and blend until the mixture is smooth.

Strain the liquid through a fine-mesh sieve into a 1-pint container (discard the solids).

Add a pinch of salt and taste for balance. Refrigerate for 1 hour to chill.

To serve, pour into martini glasses and garnish each with a carrot slice.

Cactus Cooler

Nopales, aka prickly pear cactus, are the unofficial cactus of LA. You see them everywhere from front yards to Griffith Park and they're a key ingredient in Mexican salads (once you remove the thorns and peel the paddles!). They have a great fresh flavor and silky texture. We sweeten nopales with pineapple and add mild Anaheim chile, which has all the chile flavor of a jalapeño or serrano but without the bite.

½ teaspoon coriander seeds

1 nopal pad, spines removed, peeled, and sliced (½ to ⅔ cup)

1 (6-ounce) can pineapple juice

3 tablespoons sliced fresh Anaheim chile

1 teaspoon fresh lime juice

4 teaspoons sugar

Salt

Ice

In a small dry skillet, toast the coriander seeds over medium heat until they are warm and fragrant, 2 to 3 minutes.

Set aside a couple of slices of nopal to use as garnish. Place the remainder in a blender and add the toasted coriander seeds, 16 ounces (2 cups) water, the pineapple juice, chile, lime juice, and sugar and blend until smooth.

Strain the juice through a fine-mesh sieve into 1-quart container (discard any solids).

Add a pinch of salt and taste. Cover and store the container in the fridge until ready to serve.

To serve, pour into ice-filled Collins glasses and garnish with some of the reserved nopal slices.

Banana Champurrado

Makes
SIX 8-OUNCE SERVINGS

Champurrado, a type of Mexican hot chocolate, is one of the most traditional Mexican drinks. It's like a warm hug from your grandma. It's super homey and nostalgic and great for parties. Ours is different because it has banana in it, and banana and chocolate are great buddies. Steeping the banana peels in milk extracts even more flavor from the banana. The addition of masa harina gives it that corn flour flavor and uniquely rich texture.

- **16 ounces (2 cups) milk**
- **1 organic banana, washed and peeled, peel set aside**
- **1 cinnamon stick**
- **½ cup sugar**
- **2 tablets Abuelita Mexican Hot Chocolate**
- **¾ cup masa harina**
- **Salt**
- **Cinnamon, for garnish**

In a medium pot, bring the milk to a gentle simmer over medium-high heat. Add the peeled banana and its peel. Adjust the heat so the mixture maintains a low simmer for 5 minutes, being careful not to boil and scald the milk. Remove the pot from the heat and let the milk steep until cool.

Meanwhile, in a small dry skillet, toast the cinnamon stick over medium-high heat until warm and fragrant, 2 to 3 minutes.

When the milk has cooled, strain it through a fine-mesh sieve into a large pot (discard the solids).

Add 32 ounces (4 cups) water, the sugar, and the cinnamon to the banana-infused milk. Bring to a low boil, stirring frequently to dissolve the sugar. Reduce the heat to a simmer, add the chocolate, and stir occasionally to help dissolve.

In a medium bowl, whisk together 16 ounces (2 cups) water and the masa harina until there are no clumps.

Set a fine-mesh sieve over the pot with the chocolate-milk mixture and pour the masa harina liquid through it (discard any solids).

Increase the heat to medium-high and continue to stir. When it begins to boil, reduce the heat to low and simmer for 5 minutes, stirring occasionally.

Add a pinch of salt and taste for balance. Adjust if necessary. Remove from the heat.

To serve, ladle the champurrado into a teacup or coffee mug and garnish with a light dusting of cinnamon. This can be served hot or cold.

Blueberry Muffin

This is one project that's worth the time, an insanely delicious drink that reminds me of a blueberry-corn muffin. Charring the corn makes it come alive. Serve this when it's summer and corn is at its sweetest. This is a fun drink to make with kids, and they are guaranteed to love it because it sorta tastes like Cap'n Crunch!

1 ear of corn, husked

½ ounce (1 tablespoon) fresh lime juice

3 tablespoons Blueberry Compote (recipe follows)

Salt

Ice

1 tablespoon blueberries and/or charred corn, for garnish

In a grill or over a gas stovetop burner, carefully char the ear of corn until the kernels are warm, fragrant, and slightly charred. When the cob has cooled enough to handle, use a serrated knife and carefully remove the charred corn kernels by running the knife down the sides of the cob. Discard the cob and, if desired, set aside 8 kernels for garnish.

In a blender, combine the corn, 16 ounces (2 cups) water, the lime juice, and blueberry compote and blend until the mixture is smooth.

Strain the juice through a fine-mesh sieve into a 1-quart container (discard any solids).

Add a pinch of salt and taste for balance, adjusting if necessary.

To serve, pour into ice-filled glasses and garnish with a few fresh blueberries and/or kernels of charred corn.

BLUEBERRY COMPOTE

MAKES ABOUT 1½ CUPS

Blueberry jam doesn't hold a candle to this super-simple compote made with fresh blueberries.

1 (6-ounce) container blueberries

1 cup sugar

In a saucepan, combine the berries, 4 ounces (½ cup) water, and the sugar. Bring to a simmer over medium heat, stirring occasionally. Cook until the berries break down, about 10 minutes.

Remove from the heat and allow the mixture to cool. Transfer to a blender and process until smooth.

Set a small fine-mesh sieve over a 1-pint container. Pour in the blueberry puree and press with a spoon (discard any solids). Cover and store in the fridge until ready to use.

Macho Michelada

This beer-free michelada has so much flavor you could almost serve this as a first course at dinner! You've got briny Clamato, salty umami-packed soy sauce, and savory Worcestershire—and so much more. The tortilla brine is a nice touch, but you can leave it out if you want. You definitely need a sieve for this one, because you're going to blitz all the ingredients up in a blender, including the chiles. This is a great drink to serve for guests at brunch or when you've got a crowd coming over to watch a game.

¼ teaspoon coriander seeds

8 ounces (1 cup) Clamato

⅔ ounce (4 teaspoons) fresh lime juice

½ teaspoon Worcestershire sauce

½ teaspoon soy sauce

1 teaspoon Tortilla-Infused Olive Brine (recipe follows), optional

½ dried morita chile, seeded and sliced

½ teaspoon brown sugar

Salt

Ice

Lime wedge, celery stick, and olive, for garnish

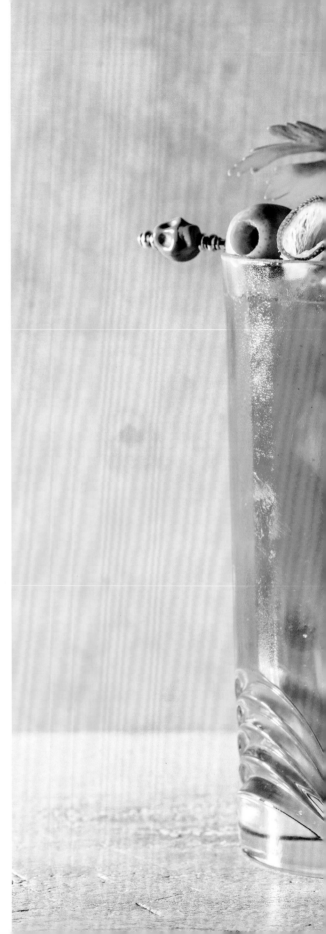

In a small dry skillet, toast the coriander seeds over medium-high heat until warm and fragrant, 2 to 3 minutes.

In a blender, combine the coriander, Clamato, lime juice, Worcestershire sauce, soy sauce, olive brine, morita chile, and brown sugar and blend until the consistency is smooth.

Strain the liquid through a fine-mesh sieve into a 1-pint container (discard any solids). Taste and adjust the seasoning if necessary. Seal and store the container in the fridge until you're ready to serve.

To serve, give the mixture a gentle stir and pour into an ice-filled tall glass. Garnish with a lime wedge, a celery stick, and an olive.

TORTILLA-INFUSED OLIVE BRINE

MAKES 8 OUNCES (1 CUP)

Corn tortillas have this magic way of giving sweet corn flavor to anything you let them steep in, like this olive brine that goes in the Macho Michelada and also the Nacho Dirty Martini (page 101).

1 corn tortilla, cut into 4 wedges

8 ounces (1 cup) olive brine

In a skillet, toast the tortilla quarters over medium heat until warm, fragrant, and slightly browned, about 3 minutes.

Transfer the tortilla quarters to a small bowl or container, add the olive brine, cover, and let sit overnight in the fridge.

Strain the mixture through a fine-mesh sieve into a 1-pint container (discard the solids). Store in the fridge until ready to use.

Paletas Frescas

Our agua frescas can double as dessert when you freeze them into paletas. For the uniniti-ated, paletas are next-level Mexican ice pops that are loaded with fresh fruit. When I was growing up, the only Mexican frozen desserts in my neighborhood were raspados, or shaved ice, made by guys carting around a big block of ice and a bunch of artificially colored fruit syrups, but these are so much better. Each recipe makes at least a dozen 3-ounce ice pops, which is the standard size of most molds in most ice-pop-making kits.

APPLE PALETAS FRESCAS

Make the Manzana Verde (page 47), leave out the club soda, and freeze according to the ice pop kit directions.

WATERMELON PALETAS FRESCAS

Make the Trejopache (page 50) and freeze according to the ice pop kit directions.

CREAMY HORCHATA PALETAS FRESCAS

Make the Morchata (page 53) and freeze according to the ice pop kit directions.

GRAPEFRUIT PALETAS FRESCAS

Make the Grapefruit Expectations (page 51), omitting the water, and freeze according to the ice pop kit directions.

TANGY TAMARIND PALETAS FRESCAS

Make the Tamarind Agua Fresca (page 60), but reduce the water to 2 cups, then freeze according to the ice pop kit directions.

BANANA CHAMPURRADO PALETAS FRESCAS

Make the Banana Champurrado (page 76) and freeze according to the ice pop kit directions.

SPICED PEAR PALETAS FRESCAS

Make the Fall Guy (page 65) and freeze according to the ice pop kit directions.

PAPAYA CILANTRO PALETAS FRESCAS

Make the Papaya and Cilantro Agua Fresca (page 70) and freeze according to the ice pop kit directions.

BLUEBERRY PALETAS FRESCAS

Make the Blueberry Muffin (page 79) and freeze according to the ice pop kit directions.

Cantina
COCK

TAILS

What's a guy like me who hasn't had a drink in fifty-plus years doing talking about cocktails? Cocktails are a big part of cantina culture, are on the menu at Trejo's Cantinas, and are a long and storied part of the history of Los Angeles. For me it's sorta like watching the Olympics or the rodeo: I'm never in my life going to get on a bobsled going 100 miles down an ice track or ride a pissed-off bull, but I sure do enjoy the stories behind the people who made it their business to be at the top of their game. My hometown is one of the greatest cocktail cities in the world, and Trejo's Cantina is now a part of this century-old tradition (see Once Upon a Cocktail in Hollywood: A Timeline, page 92).

While people can drink cocktails and live a long and productive life full of love, health, and clarity, I'm just not one of those people. I haven't had a drink for more than fifty-three years and wouldn't trade those years for the world. I'm not anti-drinking, I'm anti-me drinking! If you are one of those people who does enjoy a cocktail, then you're going to love these. Yes, we've got margaritas, and we've got a daiquiri, and takes on Manhattans and old-fashioneds.

Be Cool

I'm only going to ask you to promise me one thing: If you're going to drink, do it responsibly. Which means don't drink too much, and make it a steadfast personal rule to never get behind the wheel of a car if you've had. Even. One. Sip. Of. Alcohol. Always line up a designated driver or a plan for how to get home.

Tattoo Ink

Makes
1 COCKTAIL

My tattoos are a record of my life and an homage to the people in it. This drink is a toast to them. I've got to credit my tattoos, so activated charcoal not only gives this drink its dramatic inky black color but gives it a little body and a light toasty flavor, too.

2 teaspoons Maldon salt, for rimming the glass

Lime wedge, for rimming the glass

¾ ounce (1½ tablespoons) fresh lime juice

1 ounce (2 tablespoons) chile poblano liqueur, such as Ancho Reyes

1 ounce (2 tablespoons) mezcal

¼ teaspoon activated charcoal

½ ounce (1 tablespoon) agave syrup

Ice

Spread the Maldon salt on a small plate. Rum a lime wedge around the rim of a double rocks glass and dip the rim of the glass into the salt to coat.

In a cocktail shaker, stir together the lime juice, poblano liqueur, mezcal, activated charcoal, and agave syrup. Add 1½ cups ice, seal the shaker, and shake vigorously for about 10 seconds to chill and dilute the cocktail. Strain the drink over ice into the salt-rimmed rocks glass and serve.

Ancho Mojito

Makes
1 COCKTAIL

The American South has its mint julep, and Cuba has its mojito. Minty mojitos are like summertime in a glass. Tequila and ancho liqueur make it a Mexican summer!

8 fresh mint leaves

**½ ounce
(1 tablespoon)
fresh lime juice**

**½ ounce
(1 tablespoon)
Simple Syrup
(page 54)**

**1 ounce
(2 tablespoons)
ancho chile
liqueur, such as
Ancho Reyes**

**1 ounce
(2 tablespoons)
tequila blanco**

Ice

**2 ounces (¼ cup)
club soda**

**Mint sprig,
for garnish**

In a cocktail shaker, combine the mint leaves, lime juice, simple syrup, ancho liqueur, and tequila. Using a muddler, muddle the fresh mint to release its flavors. Add 1½ cups ice, seal the shaker, and shake it vigorously for about 10 seconds to chill and dilute the cocktail. Open the shaker and add the club soda. Strain the cocktail into an ice-filled Collins glass. Garnish with a fresh sprig of mint and serve.

The Juan Collins

The Tom Collins is a simple cocktail classic that dates back to the late 1800s. Shake up some lemon, simple syrup, and gin, pour it over ice and top with club soda and you're done. Our version uses an agave syrup flavored with black pepper and cumin to give it Mexican flavor, but frankly you could use any of our genius syrups in the book or create your own!

½ ounce (1 tablespoon) fresh lemon juice

½ ounce (1 tablespoon) Black Pepper–Cumin Agave Syrup (page 51)

1½ ounces (3 tablespoons) gin

Ice

2 ounces (¼ cup) club soda

Lemon wedge and cocktail cherry, for garnish

In a cocktail shaker, combine the lemon juice, syrup, and gin. Add 1½ cups ice, seal the shaker, and shake vigorously for about 10 seconds to chill and dilute the cocktail. Open the shaker and add the club soda.

Strain the drink into an ice-filled Collins glass and garnish with a lemon wedge and cherry.

ONCE UPON A COCKTAIL IN HOLLYWOOD

A Timeline

Hollywood and cocktails have a history, and I'm not talking about Tom Cruise in the movie *Cocktail*. Far from it. Up there with the diners and classic theaters are the old Hollywood hangouts and watering holes and clubs and lounges. Just because I don't drink cocktails doesn't mean I don't love a little Hollywood cocktail lore. While I go to Musso & Frank, Hollywood's oldest restaurant, for the pot pie special on Thursday nights, other folks go for their famous martinis. That wood-paneled high-ceilinged spot with murals immortalized in the film *Once Upon a Time in Hollywood* is dripping with history. The red-jacketed waiters, the red Naugahyde booths, and the knowledge that everyone from Charlie Chaplin to William Faulkner to Raymond Chandler patronized that joint make me feel like I'm living a little bit of history myself every time I go there. LA is dripping with history.

1919 MUSSO & FRANK GRILL OPENS

My love for this place knows no bounds. It has just enough formality, but welcomes everyone. The martinis they've been slinging for one hundred years come with a little extra in a carafe tucked into a bowl of ice.

1925 THE FORMOSA HOSTS STARS AND GANGSTERS

United Artists studios used to be across from this Cantonese-themed restaurant and hosted folks like Charlie Chaplin, Douglas Fairbanks, and gangsters Mickey Cohen and Bugsy Siegel. They don't make them like this anymore.

1934 THE ZOMBIE IS BORN AT DON THE BEACHCOMBER

The super-fruity, rum-loaded Zombie (probably one of the more accurately named cocktails of all time) was invented at Don the Beachcomber on McCadden Place, just around the corner from the Chinese Theatre.

1936 TOM BERGIN'S KICKS COFFEE UP A NOTCH

Some folks say this spot was the inspiration for the show *Cheers*. Apparently Tom Bergin was a horse-racing fanatic, which is why you'll find a horseshoe-shaped bar. The walls are festooned with shamrocks of folks who imbibed the signature Irish coffee there, including Bing Crosby and Cary Grant.

1941 THE COCK 'N BULL BEGETS THE MOSCOW MULE

The Moscow Mule was invented by a group of guys, one the president of Smirnoff, at the Cock 'n Bull on Sunset Boulevard. The copper mug that the ginger beer and vodka drink is served in turned out to be a brilliant marketing tool and helped catapult the drink to fame.

1961 TIKI-TI TIME

Filipino immigrant Ray Buhen (who used to work at Don the Beachcomber) ended up opening the tiny tiki spot Tiki-Ti in Los Feliz, which remains a tiki bar institution. It's a real LA success story.

1969 HARVEY HITS THE STRIP

Invented in the 1950s and named after surfer Tom Harvey, the Harvey Wallbanger (made with vodka, orange juice, and Galliano) becomes popular on the Sunset Strip when Galliano makes the cocktail their signature drink and markets it heavily in Los Angeles.

1970 CHASEN'S ON FIRE

Over at Chasen's in West Hollywood, bartender Pepe Ruiz invented the Flame of Love cocktail for regular Dean Martin. The cocktail gets its name from the orange oils that ignite when you squeeze the peel over a match and into the drink.

1996 LOLA'S BITES THE APPLE

The Appletini, made with vodka and apple liqueur, is invented on July Fourth at Lola's in West Hollywood.

2009 THE VARNISH ARRIVES

A history-obsessed speakeasy called The Varnish opens in the back of Cole's P.E. Buffet, the classic joint that claims to have invented the French Dip sandwich. The arrival of The Varnish raises the bartending game across the city.

2016 TREJO'S TAKES THE TOWN

Trejo's Cantina opens, serving inventive margaritas for drinkers and amazing agua frescas for folks who don't drink, and joins the annals of Hollywood history.

Mexicillin

Makes
1 COCKTAIL

The Penicillin is one of the great American cocktails of the twentieth century. It was invented by bartender Sam Ross at the neospeakeasy Milk & Honey in New York City. He eventually did a tour as bartender and came to LA, where this variation of the drink was conceived to be medicine for whatever ails you.

1 (½-inch-thick) slice fresh ginger

2 ounces (¼ cup) mezcal

¾ ounce (1½ tablespoons) fresh lime juice

¾ ounce (1½ tablespoons) Honey Syrup (recipe follows)

1 (1-inch-long) thin slice of ginger, for garnish

Ice

In a cocktail shaker, combine the ginger, mezcal, lime juice, and honey syrup. Using a muddler, muddle the fresh ginger to release its flavors. Add 1½ cups ice, seal the shaker, and shake vigorously for about 10 seconds to chill and dilute the cocktail. Strain the cocktail into an ice-filled double rocks glass and serve. Garnish with the slice of ginger.

HONEY SYRUP

MAKES 1½ OUNCES
(3 TABLESPOONS)

1 ounce (2 tablespoons) honey

½ ounce (1 tablespoon) hot water

In a small bowl, combine the honey and hot water and stir until the ingredients fully meld. Allow the mixture to cool before using.

0007499394

Inspected By: Hortencia_Puentes

Sell your books at
sellbackyourBook.com!
Go to sellbackyourBook.com
and get an instant price
quote. We even pay the
shipping - see what your old
books are worth today!

Lavender Paloma

1 COCKTAIL

All the cocktail hipsters think the Paloma is some new tequila drink, but Mexicans have been drinking it for decades. This version combines tequila and mezcal in equal parts. Too much mezcal could overwhelm the subtle flavors of the lavender—not traditional, but so nice!—and cutting it with tequila calibrates the whole deal.

¼ ounce
(½ tablespoon)
fresh lime juice

¾ ounce
(1½ tablespoons)
fresh grapefruit
juice

½ ounce
(1 tablespoon)
Lavender Syrup
(recipe follows)

¾ ounce
(1½ tablespoons)
tequila blanco

¾ ounce
(1½ tablespoons)
mezcal

Ice

2 ounces (¼ cup)
club soda

Sprig of fresh
lavender,
for garnish

In a cocktail shaker, combine the lime juice, grapefruit juice, lavender syrup, tequila blanco, and mezcal. Add 1½ cups ice, seal the shaker, and shake vigorously for about 10 seconds to chill and dilute the cocktail. Open the shaker and add the club soda. Strain into an ice-filled Collins glass and garnish with the sprig of fresh lavender.

LAVENDER SYRUP

MAKES 3 CUPS

Lavender might not be Mexican, but it sure is an LA herb. Mediterranean herbs like this grow like weeds in LA, and you see lavender growing everywhere from the fancy mansions of Hancock Park to the front yards of little Spanish bungalows in East LA. It makes this town smell like a candle store on some hot summer days! I love this syrup in iced tea with a little lemon.

16 ounces (2 cups) water

1 tablespoon dried lavender

2 cups sugar

In a small pot, bring the water to a boil. Add the lavender. Remove from the heat and let the liquid steep for 10 minutes. Add the sugar and stir until it has dissolved.

Strain the syrup through a fine-mesh sieve into a container, cover, and store in the fridge until ready to use.

Avocado Piña Colada
(AKA THE GUACO-COLADA)

Makes
1 COCKTAIL

Hats off to my cocktail team for creating this, which is just about the cleverest cocktail in this chapter. I'd order this one without the booze and be happy as a tourist sitting on the beach in Cabo . . . or San Juan, Puerto Rico, for that matter. I'm into the history of this drink: It combines the flavors of the piña colada, which was invented in Puerto Rico, with, well, guacamole. Crazy idea, right? And delicious! Rich and creamy avocado is the Mexican counterpart to coconut cream, and then the sweet and tangy pineapple and lime juice lift it up, while the jalapeño gives it a spicy backbone. The salty tortilla chip garnish cracks me up.

¼ avocado

½ teaspoon chopped fresh cilantro

1 (1-inch) length jalapeño, seeded

½ ounce (1 tablespoon) fresh lime juice

½ ounce (1 tablespoon) pineapple juice

1 ounce (2 tablespoons) cream of coconut, such as Coco López

½ ounce (1 tablespoon) mezcal

1½ ounces (3 tablespoons) tequila reposado

1½ cups ice

Salt

Tortilla chip, for garnish

In a blender, combine the avocado, cilantro, jalapeño, lime juice, pineapple juice, cream of coconut, mezcal, tequila, and ice. Blend until the mixture is smooth. Taste and season with salt if necessary. Pour into a margarita glass, garnish with a tortilla chip, and serve.

Nacho Dirty Martini

Makes
1 COCKTAIL

There are a lot of stories about the origin of the martini, but I like the one about a suddenly rich miner in Martinez, California, who, during the Gold Rush, ordered a celebratory glass of Champagne at a bar. The bar didn't have any, so the bartender whipped up a Martinez Special made with gin and vermouth and the martini was supposedly born. Over the years the recipe evolved and our version is part of that history, adding tortilla-infused olive brine and an olive stuffed with nacho cheese. Cheers!

1 teaspoon nacho cheese sauce from a can or 1 small cube Monterey Jack cheese, for garnish

1 pitted green olive, for garnish

1 (¼-inch) slice jalapeño

2½ ounces (¼ cup plus 1 tablespoon) vodka

½ ounce (1 tablespoon) Tortilla-Infused Olive Brine (page 81)

1½ cups ice

Using a small offset spatula or butter knife, spread the nacho cheese sauce into the pitted olive until full. A damp paper towel can be used to clean up any excess cheese sauce. Alternately, insert the Monterey Jack cube into the pitted olive. Do this ahead of time and store in the fridge until ready to serve.

In a cocktail shaker, combine the jalapeño, vodka, and olive brine. Using a muddler, gently crush the jalapeño slice to release its flavor. Add the ice, seal the shaker, and shake vigorously for about 10 seconds to chill and dilute the martini. Strain the cocktail into a chilled martini glass and garnish with the cheese-stuffed olive.

The Mexipolitan

Makes
1 COCKTAIL

People associate the Cosmopolitan with the show *Sex and the City* so much we almost called our spin on it Mex and the City. I love cranberry juice, and our delicious Mexican-spiced cranberry juice is what takes this version over the top.

½ ounce
(1 tablespoon)
fresh lime juice

1 ounce
(2 tablespoons)
Mexican-Spiced
Cranberry Juice
(page 69)

¼ ounce
(½ tablespoon)
Simple Syrup
(page 54)

½ ounce
(1 tablespoon)
triple sec

1½ ounces
(3 tablespoons)
vodka

1½ cups ice

Lime wedge,
for garnish

In a cocktail shaker, combine the lime juice, cranberry juice, simple syrup, triple sec, and vodka. Add the ice, seal the shaker, and shake vigorously for about 10 seconds to chill and dilute the cocktail. Strain into a chilled martini glass and garnish with a lime wedge.

Passion Fruit Pisco Sour

Makes
1 COCKTAIL

The pisco sour is one of the great cocktails of Latin America. The base is made from the clear South American spirit pisco, which is sort of like tequila made from grapes—similar to European grappa. Our version gets fruity floral tropical flavors from passion fruit and is of course made with egg whites for that trademark frothiness.

1 egg white

¼ ounce (½ tablespoon) fresh lime juice

¾ ounce (1½ tablespoons) passion fruit puree

¾ ounce (1½ tablespoons) Simple Syrup (page 54)

2 ounces (¼ cup) pisco

1½ cups ice

Angostura bitters, for garnish

In a cocktail shaker, combine the egg white, lime juice, passion fruit puree, simple syrup, and pisco. Seal the shaker and "dry shake" by shaking vigorously without ice for about 30 seconds to emulsify the ingredients. Add the ice to the shaker, seal, and "wet shake" vigorously for about 10 seconds to chill and dilute the cocktail. Strain the cocktail into a chilled martini glass. Garnish with a few drops of bitters on the surface of the foam, and serve.

The Chicano

Makes
1 COCKTAIL

Half the history of cocktails sounds like a scene out of a Wes Anderson movie. Originally served back in 1860 at Gaspare Campari's bar Caffè Campari in Milan, this drink used to be called the Milano Torino because it included Campari from Milan and Cinzano from Turin. During Prohibition, it became so popular with American tourists looking for a drink, they renamed it the Americano. Factor in the cost of a transatlantic crossing back then and that's one expensive cocktail! This version is spiced and spicy, thanks to what you could call "Chicano Cinzano," a pasilla-spiced vermouth.

2 ounces (¼ cup) Pasilla and Spice Vermouth (recipe follows)

2 ounces (¼ cup) Campari

2 ounces (¼ cup) club soda

Ice

½ orange slice dusted with Tajín, for garnish

In a Collins glass, combine the vermouth, Campari, and club soda. Fill the glass with ice and gently stir to incorporate the flavors. Garnish with the Tajín-dusted orange slice and serve.

PASILLA AND SPICE VERMOUTH

MAKES 16 OUNCES (2 CUPS)

Vermouth is simply wine infused with spices and other botanicals that is then fortified with neutral spirits. Just because it comes preflavored doesn't mean you can't add more flavor, which is what we've done with the additional infusion of a few tasty Mexican pantry spices.

5 allspice berries

¾ pasilla chile, sliced

⅛ teaspoon ground cumin

16 ounces (2 cups) sweet vermouth

In a small dry skillet, toast the allspice berries over medium heat until warm and fragrant, 2 to 3 minutes.

In a small saucepan, combine the toasted allspice berries, pasilla chile, cumin, and vermouth. Bring to a simmer over medium heat, then reduce the heat to low and continue to simmer for 5 minutes. Remove from the heat and allow it to cool to room temperature.

Strain the vermouth through a fine-mesh sieve into a 1-pint container (discard the solids). Close the container and store in the fridge until ready to use.

Classic Party Monster Margarita

The Chicano

Passion Fruit Pisco Sour

Classic Party Monster Margarita

Makes
1 COCKTAIL

While we typically use super-fresh juices made from seasonal fruit at Trejo's Cantina, even the snobbiest fancy-pants mixologists swear there's nothing like frozen limeade concentrate to get the texture and flavor of a margarita just right. Adding a little jalapeño and using agave syrup instead of sugar makes all the difference. This recipe serves one but it can easily be scaled up to make a batch for 3 or 6, as limeade concentrate comes in 6-ounce cans.

Kosher salt (optional), for rimming the glass

1 (½-inch) slice jalapeño

¼ ounce (½ tablespoon) fresh lime juice

¼ ounce (½ tablespoon) agave syrup

2 ounces (¼ cup) frozen limeade concentrate, such as Minute Maid

2 ounces (¼ cup) tequila blanco

1 cup ice

If rimming the glass, fill a shallow bowl with water. Pour a circle of kosher salt onto a small plate. Dip the rim of a rocks glass or margarita glass in the water, then dip it into the salt and set aside.

In a blender, combine the jalapeño, fresh lime juice, agave syrup, frozen limeade concentrate, tequila, and ice and blend until the mixture is smooth. Pour the margarita into the salt-rimmed glass and serve.

Bad Bunny

Don't let the Bloody Mary get all the glory as a vegetable-y brunch drink. This tequila-spiked drink made with our carrot agua fresca is perfect for daytime parties.

2 teaspoons agave syrup

1½ ounces (3 tablespoons) Carrot and Chile de Árbol Agua Fresca (page 74)

½ ounce (1 tablespoon) lime juice

1½ ounces (3 tablespoons) tequila blanco

1½ cups ice

In a cocktail shaker, combine the agave syrup and 1 teaspoon water and stir until blended. Add the chile de árbol carrot juice, lime juice, and tequila. Add the ice, seal the shaker, and shake vigorously for about 10 seconds to chill and dilute the cocktail. Strain the cocktail into a martini glass and serve.

Cantina Hack
THE 10-COUNT SHAKE

When we say "shake vigorously" we mean really hard, like tommy-gun, ratatatatatat fast, while you count to 10. You want the drink to chill down to super cold, the ice to mix up all the ingredients just right, and also dilute it just a little. And use the freshest, densest ice you can get. That stuff in bags at the grocery store has holes in it and will melt fast, watering down the drink too much.

Kiwi Michelada

Makes
1 COCKTAIL

Micheladas are super-flexible Mexican cocktails that let you dress up cheap beer with tasty ingredients, often tomato juice, Clamato, and Worcestershire. Our kiwi agua fresca makes this one super refreshing.

8 to 10 drops Tabasco sauce

2 turns cracked black pepper

½ ounce (1 tablespoon) fresh lime juice

½ ounce (1 tablespoon) Simple Syrup (page 54)

2 ounces (¼ cup) Killer Kiwi Agua Fresca (page 56), omitting the Jarritos soda

6 ounces (¾ cup) Mexican lager

Ice

1 slice kiwi, for garnish (optional)

In a 12-ounce beer glass, combine the Tabasco, black pepper, lime juice, simple syrup, kiwi agua fresca, and lager. Add a few handfuls of ice and gently stir the drink to chill it. Garnish with a slice of kiwi (if using) and serve.

Blanco Negroni

The classic Italian Negroni got so popular in recent years that bartenders started riffing on it to appeal to an even wider audience who don't like the bitter taste of Campari. We swapped in the mellower French aperitif Suze for the Campari, Lillet for the vermouth, and mezcal instead of gin. Velvet falernum adds a clove-y citrus note. The result is lighter in color than a classic Negroni, which is why we call it blanco!

½ ounce (1 tablespoon) gentian liqueur, such as Suze or Salers Aperitif

¼ ounce (½ tablespoon) velvet falernum

1 ounce (2 tablespoons) Lillet

1¼ ounces (2½ tablespoons) mezcal

Ice

1 lime, for zesting

In a mixing glass, combine the gentian liqueur, falernum, Lillet, and mezcal. Add ice all the way to the top of the glass and stir for about 30 seconds to chill and dilute. Strain into an ice-filled rocks glass. Using a Microplane, grate a little lime zest over the surface of the drink and serve.

Viejo Carré

Makes
1 COCKTAIL

One of New Orleans's most famous cocktails, the Vieux Carré has layers upon layers of flavor thanks to the local Peychaud's bitters, Bénédictine, and other complex ingredients. Aged tequila takes our version over the top.

2 dashes Angostura bitters

2 dashes Peychaud's bitters

¼ ounce (½ tablespoon) Bénédictine

¾ ounce (1½ tablespoons) sweet vermouth

¾ ounce (1½ tablespoons) Cognac

¾ ounce (1½ tablespoons) tequila añejo

Ice

Orange twist and cocktail cherry, for garnish

In a mixing glass, combine the Angostura bitters, Peychaud's bitters, Bénédictine, sweet vermouth, Cognac, and tequila. Add ice all the way to the top of the glass and stir for about 30 seconds to chill and dilute the drink. Strain into an ice-filled rocks glass and garnish with an orange twist and a cherry.

Apple Whiskey Cocktail

Makes
1 COCKTAIL

Simply put, this is apple pie in cocktail form and yet another reason to whip up a batch of our spiced green apple agua fresca. Plus, it's another drink that proves honey and apples are perfect partners.

½ ounce (1 tablespoon) Cinnamon-Honey Syrup (page 48)

½ ounce (1 tablespoon) fresh lemon juice

1¼ ounces (2½ tablespoons) Manzana Verde (page 47)

1¾ ounces (3½ tablespoons) whiskey

1½ cups ice

1 slice green apple dusted with ground cinnamon, for garnish

In a cocktail shaker, combine the cinnamon-honey syrup, lemon juice, manzana verde, and whiskey. Add the ice, seal the shaker, and shake vigorously for about 10 seconds to chill and dilute the cocktail. Strain into a martini or coupe glass and garnish with the cinnamon-dusted apple slice.

Tropical Chartreuse Sotol Cocktail

Makes
1 COCKTAIL

This is one of those mustache-twirling fancy mixology creations that sounds like you need an advanced degree in chemistry to make. It tastes like herbs and the tropics and comes out a beautiful emerald color. We use the Mexican distilled spirit called sotol, which pushes it into the realm of what we call Mex-ology!

½ ounce
(1 tablespoon)
fresh lime juice

1 ounce
(2 tablespoons)
pineapple juice

½ ounce
(1 tablespoon)
velvet falernum

¾ ounce
(1½ tablespoons)
green Chartreuse

¾ ounce
(1½ tablespoons)
sotol

Ice

Sprig of mint,
for garnish

In a cocktail shaker, combine the lime juice, pineapple juice, velvet falernum, Chartreuse, and sotol. Add 1½ cups ice, seal the shaker, and shake vigorously for about 10 seconds to chill and dilute the drink. Strain into an ice-filled double rocks glass and garnish with the mint sprig.

Watermelon Man

Makes
1 COCKTAIL

This refreshing and easy cocktail is beautifully and vividly pink (almost like the boxes at Trejo's Donut's!)—perfect for celebrations. But it lives or dies on the quality of watermelon, which means you're going to have to make it in the summer months, when watermelon is at its sweet peak.

¼ ounce
(½ tablespoon)
fresh lime juice

½ ounce
(1 tablespoon)
Simple Syrup
(page 54)

2 ounces (¼ cup)
Watermelon Agua
Fresca (page 66)

½ ounce
(1 tablespoon)
vodka

1 ounce
(2 tablespoons) gin

Ice

1 watermelon slice,
for garnish

In a cocktail shaker, combine the lime juice, simple syrup, watermelon agua fresca, vodka, and gin. Add 1½ cups ice, seal the shaker, and shake vigorously for about 10 seconds to chill and dilute the drink. Strain into an ice-filled rocks glass and garnish with a slice of watermelon.

Viejo Vato

Makes
1 COCKTAIL

The Old Pal was supposedly invented at Harry's New York Bar at the Ritz in Paris, where Ernest Hemingway used to tear it up back in the day. It's one of those super-easy three-ingredient drinks made from equal parts rye whiskey, dry vermouth, and Campari. Instead of rye we use tequila reposado, which is slightly aged, and takes it into cantina territory.

¾ ounce
(1½ tablespoons)
dry vermouth

1½ ounces
(3 tablespoons)
tequila reposado

¾ ounces
(1½ tablespoons)
Campari

Ice

Orange twist,
for garnish

In a mixing glass, combine the vermouth, tequila, and Campari. Fill the glass with ice and stir for about 30 seconds to chill and dilute the cocktail. Strain into a chilled martini or coupe glass and garnish with an orange twist.

To Live and Rye in L.A.

The whiskey sour is an American cocktail classic. We turn it into a flip, the egg white–based cocktail preparation that shakes up creamy and frothy, which also helps transmit the sweet corn flavor of our tortilla–infused rye. For a super–simple variation, skip the egg white—it'll be just as good.

1 egg white

¾ ounce (1½ tablespoons) fresh lemon juice

¾ ounce (1½ tablespoons) Simple Syrup (page 54)

2 ounces (¼ cup) Tortilla-Infused Rye Whiskey (recipe follows)

1½ cups ice

In a cocktail shaker, combine the egg white, lemon juice, simple syrup, and rye. Seal the shaker and "dry shake" by shaking vigorously without ice for about 20 seconds to emulsify the ingredients. Add the ice to the shaker, seal, and "wet shake" vigorously for about 20 seconds to chill and dilute the cocktail. Strain into a martini or coupe glass.

TORTILLA-INFUSED RYE WHISKEY

MAKES 1 (750 ML) BOTTLE

Infusing rye whiskey with corn tortillas is brilliant: Rye is often distilled from corn and steeping toasted corn tortillas doubles up the sweet corn flavor.

4 corn tortillas

1 (750 ml) bottle rye whiskey

In a large skillet, toast the tortillas until they are warm, blistered, and fragrant. Cut the tortillas into quarters. In a large pitcher or container, combine the whiskey and tortillas, cover, and refrigerate for 24 hours.

Discard the tortillas and strain the whiskey through a fine-mesh sieve back into its bottle. Label and store in the fridge until ready to use.

The Los Angeles

Makes
1 COCKTAIL

The Manhattan is one of the American cocktail kings, whether you're ordering one in a temple of mixology or a corner dive. We swapped in our pasilla-spiced vermouth to give it more Angeleno intrigue and named it after the other great metropolis of the Americas that I call home. If you like a drier cocktail, scale back the vermouth and use more bourbon.

1 barspoon agave syrup (a little less if you prefer a drier cocktail)

4 to 8 dashes Angostura bitters

1½ ounces (3 tablespoons) Pasilla and Spice Vermouth (page 105)

1½ ounces (3 tablespoons) bourbon

1½ cups ice

Cocktail cherry and/ or orange twist, for garnish

In a mixing glass, combine the agave syrup, bitters, vermouth, and bourbon. Add the ice and stir for about 30 seconds to chill and dilute the drink. Strain into a martini or coupe glass and garnish with a cherry, an orange twist, or both.

Tequila Old-Fashioned

Makes
1 COCKTAIL

Thank the popularity of the TV series *Mad Men* for the massive enthusiasm for the old-fashioned. It also helps that the drink is just sweet enough without being *too* sweet. We use our smoky-spicy and supremely delicious chipotle syrup to add the sweet note and substitute aged tequila to play the part of full-flavored bourbon.

2 dashes mole bitters (we like Bittermens Xocolatl Mole Bitters)

4 dashes Angostura bitters

⅛ ounce (¾ teaspoon) Chipotle Syrup (page 64)

2 ounces (¼ cup) Tequila Añejo or Extra Añejo

Ice

1 orange twist and a cocktail cherry, for garnish

In a rocks glass, combine both bitters, the chipotle syrup, and tequila. Add enough ice to fill up the glass and gently stir for about 30 seconds to chill and dilute the drink. Garnish with a twist of orange and a cherry and serve.

The Lime in the Coconut

Makes
1 COCKTAIL

This bubbly rum tropical cocktail combines the classic flavor of lime and coconut, just like the song says.

2 lime wedges

½ ounce (1 tablespoon) coconut rum

1½ ounces (3 tablespoons) tequila

4 ounces (½ cup) Sprite

Ice

1 lime slice, for garnish

In a Collins glass, combine the lime wedges, coconut rum, and tequila. Using a muddler, muddle the limes to release the juices and the oils from the peel. Top with the Sprite and add enough ice to fill up the glass. Garnish with a slice of lime.

Whiskey Coke Cassis

Makes
1 COCKTAIL

Insiders know to use Mexican-produced Coca-Cola, aka "Mexicoke," which is made with cane sugar instead of high-fructose corn syrup and has a more pronounced flavor. Crème de cassis has a dark berry flavor. Add a shot of whiskey to turn this into an adults-only cherry Coke.

2 lemon wedges

½ ounce (1 tablespoon) crème de cassis

1½ ounces (3 tablespoons) whiskey

4 ounces (½ cup) Mexican Coca-Cola

Ice

1 lemon slice and 2 cocktail cherries, for garnish

In a Collins glass, combine the lemon wedges, crème de cassis, and whiskey. Using a muddler, muddle the lemon to release the juices and the oils from the peel. Top with Coke, add ice, and garnish with a lemon slice and cherries.

Strawberry Fanta-sy Jalapeño

Makes
1 COCKTAIL

While we usually use fresh fruit when making our cocktails at the cantina, sometimes nothing beats that nostalgic childhood flavor of strawberry soda.

1 slice jalapeño

1 lime wedge

1½ ounces (3 tablespoons) tequila blanco

4 ounces (½ cup) strawberry soda, preferably Fanta

Ice

1 lime slice, for garnish

In a Collins glass, combine the jalapeño and lime wedge. Using a muddler, muddle them together. Add the tequila. Top with the strawberry soda and add enough ice to fill up the glass. Garnish with the lime slice.

SAUCES, and

SALSAS, DIPS

When I was growing up nobody would buy pre-made salsa, they always made their own. Even hot sauce. If someone caught you with a bottle of Tapatío, you'd get laughed at! My mom was known for making the hottest pico de gallo in the world, but she also knew some people just want the flavor, not the heat, so she'd make mild and semihot, as well as her infamous "go to hell" version, too. Sometimes the hottest would be so fiery I swear it would knock your teeth out! My dad used to say "Don't eat this, Danny. This is for real men." And, of course, wanting to prove myself, I'd lean right in and say "Dammit, give it to me!" And in a few bites I'd be sweating and burning with the best of them, which was so stupid because I couldn't enjoy my meal with my mouth on fire. Eventually trying to prove myself got so painful I had to stop eating with my dad altogether.

Today I like my salsa medium-hot because I still want to taste my food. And that's what the salsas, sauces, and dips in this chapter are all about: easy and delicious ways to upgrade whatever else you're eating. They've got just the right amount of heat or brightness, or tangy lime, rich crema, or cheese to make a snack into a meal, and to take a taco or tostada over the top.

Like the other dishes in this book, these sauces are starting points, so you should always taste them while preparing, and adjust them as you like. If you think something needs more heat, double up the jalapeño. If you want to use the Mexican Thousand Island Dressing (page 140) on a tuna sandwich, do it! The creamy Elote Salsa (page 146) is great straight up on a chip, but a scoop of it in a midweek green salad is a great idea, too. And honestly, mix it with some leftover penne pasta and, heck, you've got a fine pasta salad. Versatility is everything! Which is why we've shared ideas for using the recipe in other ways.

As you cook your way through this chapter you'll probably find yourself with more than a couple favorites. My advice: Make a couple at a time to use through the rest of the week to enliven any meal. They could just as easily say "Variety is the salsa of life." And of course if you want to be like my mom and earn a reputation for burning peoples' teeth out, do your family and friends a favor and put a little sign up by the bowl that says "Do not eat this salsa!"

Queso Fundido

Serves **6 TO 8**

Queso fundido is the undisputed world champion of cheesy dips, fondue be damned. Topped with spicy-savory chorizo and served with crunchy tortilla chips, it's a knockout-delicious appetizer. While we typically use organic and artisanal products at our restaurants, sometimes you need to add a secret ingredient to take a dish over the top. In this case it's Velveeta, which is neither organic nor artisanal! While it might not be the first thing you think of when you're cooking Mexican food, it helps keep the other cheeses smooth and melted and from getting all stringy and gloppy.

1 tablespoon neutral oil, such as canola

5 ounces fresh chorizo, removed from casings

¼ cup plus 2 tablespoons diced white onion

1 large garlic clove, minced

1 cup half-and-half

6 ounces Velveeta, roughly chopped (from 8 slices)

2½ cups shredded Mexican cheese blend

1 (4-ounce) can chopped Hatch chiles

1 tablespoon chopped canned chipotle peppers in adobo sauce

1 teaspoon dried oregano

1 teaspoon chili powder

2 tablespoons chopped fresh cilantro

Tortilla chips or warm corn tortillas, for serving

In a medium skillet, warm the canola oil over medium heat until it begins to shimmer, about 2 minutes. Add the chorizo and cook, stirring occasionally, until it's fully cooked and crumbly, about 10 minutes. Remove the chorizo from the pan and set aside.

Add ¼ cup of the onion and the garlic to the pan and cook, stirring occasionally, until they are soft and translucent, about 4 minutes. Return the chorizo to the pan and cook for 3 more minutes, stirring occasionally. Remove the pan from the heat and set aside.

In a large heavy saucepan, combine the half-and-half and Velveeta and cook over medium heat, stirring occasionally, until the Velveeta is melted, 6 to 8 minutes. Add the Mexican cheese blend and stir until the cheese has melted and the mixture is smooth, about 3 minutes. Mix in the Hatch chiles, chipotle pepper, oregano, and chili powder.

Transfer the melted queso to a warm dish or cast-iron pan and top with the reserved chorizo-onion mixture, remaining 2 tablespoons diced onion, and the cilantro. Serve immediately with tortilla chips or warm corn tortillas.

Avocado Salsa

Makes about
2 CUPS

From Olvera Street taquito joints to mini-mall taco stands to food trucks cranking out al pastor, offering avocado salsa at your condiment bar is what sets the great apart from the good. A little rich, a little tangy, and slightly spicy, this is a fantastic salsa that's great for dipping chips, drizzling over taquitos or empanadas, or topping whatever taco you're cooking up.

2 avocados, roughly chopped

4 medium tomatillos (about ½ pound), stemmed, papery husk removed, and quartered

¼ cup packed fresh cilantro leaves

½ medium white onion, roughly chopped

½ jalapeño, roughly chopped

2 medium garlic cloves, peeled

Juice of 2 limes

1 teaspoon kosher salt, plus more to taste

In a blender, combine the avocados, tomatillos, cilantro, onion, jalapeño, garlic, lime juice, 6 tablespoons water, and the salt and blend until smooth, 1 to 2 minutes. If the salsa is too thick, add a splash more water and blend again. Continue to adjust until you reach the desired consistency. Taste the salsa and add more salt to taste.

Roasted Jalapeño Chimichurri

Makes about
1½ CUPS

The Argentinians know a thing or two about grilled meats, and their herby garlic chimichurri sauce stands up to a perfectly grilled piece of steak. We've added some smoky toasty spicy flavors to our version with fire-roasted jalapeños and bell peppers for color. The trick to making it just the right consistency is the addition of lightly salted water: This thins out the sauce and keeps it from being too tangy or too oily. While we serve it with our grilled skirt steak later in the book (see Arrachera Steak, page 206), it's great on grilled fish and poultry, too.

1 medium jalapeño, left whole

1 small red bell pepper, left whole

1 teaspoon kosher salt

6 garlic cloves, minced

6 cherry tomatoes, finely chopped

1 bunch of cilantro, leaves and tender stems (about 2 cups loosely packed), finely chopped

2 teaspoons dried oregano

Juice of 2 limes

Juice of 1 orange

½ cup extra virgin olive oil

Over an open flame, roast the jalapeño on all sides until its skin is charred and blackened, turning occasionally, 5 to 7 minutes. Allow the jalapeño to cool, then rub off the charred skin with a paper towel. Slice the jalapeño lengthwise, remove the seeds and ribs, then finely dice. Repeat the roasting, peeling, seeding, and dicing process with the bell pepper.

In a small bowl, stir the salt into ¼ cup water. In a large bowl, combine the jalapeño, bell pepper, garlic, tomatoes, cilantro, oregano, lime juice, orange juice, salted water, and olive oil. Whisk the mixture until thoroughly combined. Transfer to a nonreactive container such as a glass jar and let the flavors combine and mellow for at least 2 hours or up to 12 hours.

Aji Sauce

Green Dipping Sauce

Roasted Jalapeño Chimichurri

Avocado Salsa

Green Dipping Sauce

Makes about
2 CUPS

This dipping sauce is custom-made for our empanadas and gets its bite from jalapeño and its tangy richness from sour cream. While cilantro is the traditional herb, some folks have a genetic quirk that makes it taste like soap to them. It's all good. There are no strict rules in Trejo town when it comes to cooking, so feel free to modify it to suit your taste—like substituting basil or flat-leaf parsley. It will be delicious.

2 cups loosely packed fresh cilantro

2 scallions, white and light-green parts only, roughly chopped

2 garlic cloves, peeled

¼ medium jalapeño, seeded and roughly chopped

Juice of 2 limes

1 tablespoon red wine vinegar

⅓ cup olive oil

½ cup sour cream

½ teaspoon kosher salt

Freshly ground black pepper

In a food processor or blender, combine the cilantro, scallions, garlic, jalapeño, lime juice, and vinegar and pulse to combine, scraping down the sides as needed with a rubber spatula to bring ingredients closer to the blade. Pulse again, for about 30 seconds, or until finely chopped. With the machine running, add the olive oil in a slow stream until the mixture is well combined. Add the sour cream and mix well until incorporated and smooth. Add the salt and season with black pepper to taste. Taste and adjust the seasonings.

Ají Sauce

Makes about
1½ CUPS

In strip malls and parking lots across LA, you'll see red-tinged grilled and rotisserie chicken cooked "a la brasa" in the Peruvian style. It's always served with this spicy and garlicky green sauce that gets some of its briny punch from Cotija cheese. It's the perfect accompaniment to succulent charred and grilled meats.

½ cup mayonnaise

1 bunch of fresh cilantro

2 medium jalapeños, halved and seeded

3 garlic cloves, roughly chopped

¼ cup crumbled Cotija cheese

2 tablespoons fresh lime juice, plus more to taste

½ teaspoon kosher salt, plus more to taste

In a blender, combine the mayonnaise, cilantro, jalapeños, garlic, Cotija, lime juice, and salt and blend until smooth, about 1 minute. Taste and add more salt or lime juice, if desired.

Mexican Thousand Island Dressing

Makes about
1 CUP

Thousand Island dressing is one of mankind's highest achievements in the category of "Is it a dressing, or is it dip?" Whatever it is, it's delicious and we've managed to make it even better with the adobo sauce from that can't-fail Mexican culinary turbocharger known as canned chipotles, the smoky and spicy, slightly sweet secret ingredient in so many of our recipes. Adding chopped pickled jalapeños, cilantro, and lime makes the dressing Mexican-ish and maybe one of the tastiest and easiest recipes in this book. We recommend it on hamburgers or hot dogs . . . or straight from the bowl on a chip.

- ¾ cup mayonnaise
- 2 tablespoons ketchup
- 1 tablespoon adobo sauce from canned chipotle peppers in adobo sauce
- ¼ cup minced pickled jalapeños
- ¼ cup minced white onion
- ¼ teaspoon kosher salt
- Juice of ½ lime
- ¼ cup finely chopped fresh cilantro leaves

In a large bowl, combine the mayonnaise, ketchup, adobo sauce, pickled jalapeños, onion, salt, lime juice, and cilantro. Mix well to thoroughly combine.

HOLLYWOOD
Forever

Anybody who knows me knows that I'm never at a loss for words, but one night in Hollywood on the roof of Madame Tussauds wax museum I was speechless. There I was up on the stage waiting for a life-size wax replica of myself to be unveiled. Yep, a shockingly realistic shirt-less version of me immortalized in painted paraffin in the grand tradition of movie stars like Robert De Niro, John Wayne, Clint Eastwood, and dozens of others on display in this iconic Hollywood institution. The irony of it all was not lost on me. I used to come to Hollywood to hide from the cops, and now here I was being honored. I was feeling pretty damned emotional.

Out in the crowd were hundreds of friends, and family members, and people I'd worked with over the years. Actors, producers, writers, stunt men, ex-cons I'd done time with and a U.S. congressman, my agents, my business partners, my trusted staff, and none other than the mayor of Los Angeles. The legendary Chicano band Tierra was playing. The mayor handed me a machete (how's that for a first line of a movie?), I chopped a ribbon with it, the red curtain dropped, and there I was, looking at that badass wax version of me, shirtless, tattooed, arms raised. I was choked up.

Before the guests arrived, I wandered through the museum alone and was looking around seeing all the Latino legends in wax like George Lopez (even though the head's not big

enough—ha!) and J.Lo—it was a powerful experience. I also saw Charlie Chaplin, Charles Bronson, and all these other people who I idolized. And then it hit me. "I'm here, too." Being put in Madame Tussauds wax museum is sort of like a lifetime achievement award. Before the party started I sat in the greenroom and I looked out over Hollywood. I could see the long road to how I got here.

Down the street is Grauman's Chinese, where I used to go to see movies as a kid with whatever money I could scrape together. My movies premiere there now—I walk the red carpet there now. Around the corner is the Cinerama Dome, which I helped build. There's Hollywood Forever Cemetery, the classic cemetery that is a good reminder of everyone who comes before us and a reminder to make the most of every moment you have.

Back in the sixties when we used to cruise around town at night, we'd start in the Valley on Van Nuys Boulevard, drive down to Whittier, and always end up back on Hollywood Boulevard. Hollywood Forever was where couples would go. They didn't used to lock the gates, so you could drive right in. At two or three in the morning, there'd be all kinds of cars parked there. Now that I've got some years on me, I see it as a place where we go to honor the dead and celebrate the living. When you go to Rome, and you go into the cathedrals, you can't help being overwhelmed. Whatever you believe or don't believe, it doesn't matter, it's just the history there. It's the same thing at Hollywood Forever. You go around and look at graves and see the obscure and the famous people buried there like Cecil B. DeMille, Rudolph Valentino, and O.G. Angeleno

Bugsy Siegel. It's a full-circle place that anybody who wants to take the long view on life and fame should visit. And it's just a beautiful place, with trees and rolling hills and peacocks wandering the grounds. I used to go there with my kids to see movies they'd project on a mausoleum with everybody picnicking on the lawn. We had the premiere of *The Devil's Rejects* there with Rob Zombie. And my best friend Eddie Bunker is buried there.

Eddie was an ex-con and screenwriter who helped me get my start in the movies and liked to write late at night. He lived on McCadden Place and when he had writer's block he'd call me and I'd drive over. We'd take late-night walks up and down the side streets and boulevards when everyone else was asleep. I love that if you visit Hollywood, there's so much history that you can always take the long view and see the layers. Sometimes at the end of one of our long walks we'd go to the Denny's not far from Hollywood Forever across the parking lot from a strip mall they call Gower Gulch. We'd sit and eat our pancakes and Eddie would tell me stories of how back before we were there real cowboys who wanted to get work as extras on movies at the nearby studios would come with their horses and stand around hoping they'd get cast in movies and TV shows, and that's how the little shopping mall got the name Gower Gulch.

I was comforted by the fact that no matter what happens in the future, after I'm long gone, I'll always be in Hollywood, in the wax museum not far from Hollywood Forever, with so many of my heroes and friends, and some kid will be inspired to shoot for the moon, just like I did, and like so many before me did, too.

Crunchy Salsa Macha

Makes about
2 CUPS

Crunchy, spicy, seedy, and toasty salsa macha is one of those Mexican culinary creations that's been trending recently as folks in the US explore the lesser-known regions of Mexico. It's a staple of Veracruz and Oaxaca and is less tangy and a lot more earthy than other salsas. It's great with grilled meats and fish and adds a nice crunchy texture to whatever you decide to top or dip.

2 ancho chiles

6 dried guajillo chiles

5 dried chiles de árbol

1½ cups grapeseed oil

4 garlic cloves, peeled but whole

½ cup sunflower seeds

1 teaspoon dried oregano

1½ teaspoons kosher salt, plus more to taste

2 tablespoons apple cider vinegar, plus more to taste

2½ teaspoons light brown sugar

Slice open the ancho, guajillo, and árbol chiles and remove the stems and seeds. Roughly chop the chiles and set them aside.

In a medium saucepan, heat the oil over medium-low heat. Add the garlic cloves and cook until they turn slightly golden, 2 to 3 minutes, being careful not to burn them. Add the chiles and sunflower seeds. Cook, stirring often, for 3 to 5 minutes. You want the ingredients to cook and infuse the oil with their flavor but not toast or get bitter. Adjust the heat as necessary to keep the mixture from burning. The oil should gently sizzle but not crackle or get smoky. Remove the pan from the heat, stir in the oregano, and let the mixture cool for about 15 minutes.

Transfer the mixture to a blender. Add the salt, vinegar, and brown sugar. Blend until smooth. Taste and add more salt and vinegar if needed. Transfer the salsa to a glass jar, let cool, and refrigerate for up to 2 weeks.

Elote Salsa

Makes about
4½ CUPS

The flavors of elote—the famous street corn served from carts throughout LA and in our Trejo's restaurants as a salad—make an amazing creamy-spicy dip that tastes like pure summer. While most elote is made with steamed or boiled corn, this elote salsa is made with fresh corn kernels toasted in a hot skillet until slightly charred so that it tastes smoky as well.

3 ears corn, kernels sliced off (about 4 cups)

¼ cup crumbled Cotija cheese

¼ cup finely diced red onion

¼ cup mayonnaise

¼ cup chopped fresh cilantro

1 tablespoon finely diced jalapeño

Juice of ½ lime, plus more to taste

¼ teaspoon chili powder, plus more to taste

Kosher salt

In a large skillet, cook the corn kernels over medium heat, stirring occasionally, until they turn a deep butter yellow and become light brown in spots, about 10 minutes. Remove from the heat and let the kernels cool.

In a large bowl, combine the corn, Cotija, red onion, mayonnaise, cilantro, jalapeño, lime juice, and chili powder and stir until combined. Taste for seasoning and add salt if needed, or more lime juice or chili powder.

Chipotle Lime Crema

Flavored cremas are a staple of the Trejo's Tacos menu and add zip and richness to so many bowls, tacos, and burritos. If you don't already have a copy of the *Trejo's Tacos* cookbook, I highly recommend you pick it up to learn those crema recipes and other tricks of the restaurant. This crema is like our popular lime crema but with a dose of chipotle to give it spice. It's a great tostada topper and goes well with the tuna tostadas later in the book (see page 191), but don't let that stop you from slathering it on sandwiches or drizzling it on tacos.

1 cup sour cream

2 tablespoons adobo sauce from canned chipotle peppers in adobo sauce

1 tablespoon fresh lime juice

¼ teaspoon kosher salt

In a medium bowl, combine the sour cream, adobo sauce, lime juice, and salt and stir to combine.

Habanero Tartar Sauce

Makes about
1¼ CUPS

Frying was my mom's preferred method of making fish and seafood in our house when I was a kid. Even though we mostly ate Mexican food, tartar sauce was all the rage back in the 1950s and '60s. This recipe combines my nostalgia for that classic tartar with the power of Mexican chiles, particularly the high-octane hit of habanero.

1 cup mayonnaise

1 tablespoon Dijon mustard

1 medium shallot, minced

2 tablespoons diced dill pickle

2 tablespoons diced pickled jalapeño

1 teaspoon minced habanero chile

2 tablespoons finely chopped fresh cilantro

Juice of 1 lime

½ teaspoon kosher salt

Freshly ground black pepper

Several dashes hot sauce, such as Tapatío or Cholula

1 teaspoon adobo sauce from canned chipotle peppers in adobo sauce

In a medium bowl, combine the mayonnaise, mustard, shallot, dill pickle, pickled jalapeño, habanero, cilantro, lime juice, salt, black pepper, hot sauce, and adobo sauce. Stir to combine. Refrigerate for up to 4 days.

Badass Blender Salsa

Makes about
4 CUPS

Sure you could buy "fresh" salsa in a little plastic tub at the supermarket. Or you could make it a weekly ritual to blitz up a batch of blender salsa every week and use it on tacos, with chips and guacamole, or even with crudités. While I'm a big proponent of using fresh vegetables, canned tomatoes are preferable here because they're less watery and have a consistent deep tomato flavor.

1 (28-ounce) can whole peeled tomatoes with their juices

1 cup loosely packed fresh cilantro

½ medium white onion, roughly chopped

2 medium jalapeños, seeded and roughly chopped

2 garlic cloves, roughly chopped

1 teaspoon kosher salt

Juice of 2 limes

2 canned chipotle peppers in adobo sauce

In a blender, combine the tomatoes, cilantro, onion, jalapeños, garlic, salt, lime juice, and chipotles and process until smooth. Store refrigerated for up to 5 days.

Pico de Gallo

Makes about
3 CUPS

Here's another go-to salsa to keep on hand and pretty much put on everything for a boost of fresh spicy flavor. This is one of those recipes you're going to taste and tweak. No two fresh tomatoes taste the same, so you might need to add a little more salt or lime to get the flavor balance just right. Peak of summer heirloom tomatoes are always going to taste best, but for the rest of the year we like to use those vine tomatoes sold on the stem.

2 medium tomatoes, diced

½ small red onion, diced

½ small white onion, diced

2 jalapeños, halved, seeds and ribs removed, diced

¼ cup chopped fresh cilantro

Juice of 1 lime, plus more to taste

1 tablespoon olive oil

1 teaspoon kosher salt, plus more to taste

In a medium bowl, combine the tomatoes, both onions, the jalapeños, cilantro, lime juice, olive oil, and salt and mix well. Taste and add more salt or lime juice if desired.

SNACKS
and
SIDES

If you're like me, sometimes you just want to stand in the kitchen, wrap something in a tortilla, and call it lunch. Other times you want to sit down to a proper, bona fide, real-deal meal. To me, it's the difference between eating and dining. And that's what the recipes in this chapter do: They turn food into a feast. Here you'll find beans that taste like abuela's that, when paired with brightly colored super-green rice make whatever you combine them with the combo platter of your dreams. We've got the ultimate carnitas-smothered nachos with just the right ratio of cheese to spice to crunch, and deviled eggs that use not one but three kinds of chiles to make them diabolically delicious. You'll also find our take on a Caesar salad and a tangy/spicy coleslaw—both will have you gobbling up your vegetables. And while I don't eat much dessert these days, when I do I make it count with Chai-Spiced Apple Empanadas that remind me of my childhood, but with a grown-up twist.

Diablo Eggs

Makes
16 DEVILED EGGS

Deviled eggs are an American party classic. Growing up, I remember always seeing them at birthday parties, christenings, and quinceañeras alongside a cross-cultural buffet of pigs in blankets, albóndigas, and tamales. While they may remind you of the suburbs, this version turns up the heat with a combination of fresh and pickled jalapeños and hot sauce.

1 tablespoon kosher salt

8 large eggs

3 tablespoons mayonnaise

2 tablespoons sour cream

2 teaspoons yellow mustard

2 tablespoons finely diced pickled jalapeños

2 tablespoons finely diced white onion

1½ teaspoons fresh lime juice

½ teaspoon ground cumin

Hot sauce, such as Cholula or Tapatío

4 tablespoons finely chopped fresh cilantro

Salt and freshly ground black pepper

1 tablespoon finely diced fresh jalapeño

Chipotle chile powder

Fill a large bowl with ice and water (you'll use this to stop your eggs from overcooking). In a medium pot, bring 4 cups water and the kosher salt to a boil. Using a spoon, carefully lower the eggs to the bottom of the pot. Reduce the heat to a simmer and cook the eggs for 10 minutes. Transfer the eggs to the ice water bath to cool down, about 5 minutes. Once they're cool enough to handle, peel the eggs.

In a medium bowl, combine the mayonnaise, sour cream, mustard, pickled jalapeños, onion, lime juice, cumin, 2 dashes of hot sauce, and 2 tablespoons of the cilantro. Season with salt and black pepper to taste.

Carefully cut the eggs in half lengthwise. Scoop out the yolks, add them to the mayonnaise mixture, and place the whites, cut side up, on a plate. Using a fork, mash the cooked yolks into the mayonnaise mixture. Season with more salt and pepper.

Fill the egg halves with the yolk mixture. Top the eggs with the diced fresh jalapeño, sprinkle with chipotle powder, hit each egg with a dash of hot sauce, and garnish with the remaining 2 tablespoons cilantro.

Grilled Mexican Caesar Salad

WITH PEPITAS

Serves **4**

The Caesar salad was invented at the Hotel Caesar in Tijuana by an Italian immigrant named Caesar Cardini, but doesn't have any Mexican ingredients in it. We decided to change that with our adaptation that adds a hit of chipotle peppers in adobo for subtle deep heat, fresh cilantro, fresh lime juice for bite, and toasty pepitas for crunch. Grilling the romaine gives it all a little char. A perfect party dish for a backyard barbecue starring Pollo Asada a la Brasa (page 184) or Arrachera Steak (page 206).

1 head romaine lettuce, quartered lengthwise

1 tablespoon olive oil

1 teaspoon kosher salt

1 teaspoon freshly ground black pepper

Caesar Dressing (recipe follows)

½ cup shaved Parmigiano-Reggiano cheese

¼ cup chopped fresh cilantro

2 tablespoons roasted pepitas (preferably unsalted)

2 limes, quartered lengthwise, for squeezing

Heat a charcoal or gas grill to medium. Brush the romaine pieces with the olive oil and season with the salt and pepper. Place the romaine cut side down on the grill and cook until slightly charred but still crisp in the center, about 2 minutes. Flip over and cook for 2 minutes more.

Place the romaine pieces cut side up on a serving platter. Drizzle with approximately ½ cup of the dressing and garnish with the shaved Parmigiano, cilantro, and pepitas. Serve with lime wedges on the side for squeezing.

CAESAR DRESSING

MAKES 1½ CUPS

This makes enough to dress two salads. Trust me, you'll want to eat this killer Caesar two days in a row!

2 medium garlic cloves, minced

2 anchovies, minced

2 tablespoons fresh lime juice

1 teaspoon fresh lemon juice

1 teaspoon Dijon mustard

1½ teaspoons adobo sauce from canned chipotle peppers in adobo sauce

1 cup mayonnaise

½ cup freshly grated Parmigiano-Reggiano cheese

Freshly ground black pepper

In a medium bowl, combine the garlic, anchovies, lime juice, lemon juice, mustard, adobo sauce, mayonnaise, Parmigiano, and black pepper to taste and whisk to combine.

Fight-Night Nachos Supreme

WITH CARNITAS

Serves **6 TO 8**

When I serve these nachos at fight nights, people get so excited that I almost have to referee access to the buffet. These are over the top, served "supreme" style, not only drizzled with sour cream but also topped with carnitas. You have to make sure you assemble the nachos so that every bite has a little bit of every topping. The trick is to make a single layer of chips first, top that layer, add another layer of chips, and then build another lighter layer on top. One of my favorite ways of eating leftover nachos is as breakfast the next day, warmed in the oven, with two eggs over easy on top.

Carnitas

1 medium orange

3 pounds boneless pork shoulder, cut into 2-inch cubes

2 teaspoons kosher salt

Freshly ground black pepper

Nachos

Cooking spray

2 (11-ounce) bags tortilla chips

2 (15-ounce) cans pinto beans, drained and rinsed

¼ cup Quick Pickled Red Onions (page 194)

2 pounds shredded Monterey Jack, Colby Jack blend, or Mexican cheese blend

2 cups sour cream

2 avocados, thinly sliced

2 cups pico de gallo, homemade (page 152) or store-bought

MAKE THE CARNITAS: Preheat the oven to 325°F.

Using a vegetable peeler or knife, cut off two 2-inch-long strips of orange zest and set aside. Cut the orange in half and squeeze the juice into a small bowl. You should have about ¼ cup.

In a Dutch oven or large ovenproof pot, spread out the cubed pork in a single layer. Sprinkle it with the salt and pepper to taste. Pour the orange juice into the pot and stir to coat the pork. Tightly cover the pot, transfer to the oven, and bake until tender, 1½ to 2 hours. Check the pork every 30 minutes. If it's sticking or drying out, add ¼ cup water. If after 2 hours the pork is still firm and not yet tender, return it to the oven for 20 minutes or so more. It will eventually become tender.

recipe continues

Increase the oven temperature to 450°F. Uncover the pot and roast for about 10 minutes until one side is browned. Turn pieces over and roast for 10 minutes more to brown the other side. At this point, the juices should have evaporated, leaving behind a nice layer of fat. Remove the pork from the oven and use two forks to smash and shred each piece of pork.

ASSEMBLE THE NACHOS: Reduce the oven temperature to 350°F. Mist two large baking sheets with cooking spray.

Dividing evenly, spread one bag of chips in the two prepared baking sheets. Top with half of the carnitas, beans, onion, and shredded cheese. Repeat the layers with the remaining bag of chips, carnitas, beans, onion, and shredded cheese. Place one sheet of nachos into the oven and bake until the cheese is melted, 20 to 25 minutes. Repeat with the second pan.

Meanwhile, stir 2 tablespoons water into the sour cream to loosen it.

Serve the nachos topped with the avocado slices, pico de gallo, and sour cream.

The Taste of Freedom

There's a rhythm to breakfast depending on where you are in life or the year. During the summertime when I was kid, the fact that you weren't going to school meant you had time for a real breakfast on weekdays, and my mom would sometimes make more elaborate meals like chorizo and eggs and chilaquiles, or migas. Sometimes we'd have rice and meat, depending on what was left over from the night before. My mom was great with leftovers. In prison, depending on the day, you'd have pancakes one day, bacon and eggs another, but they always had potatoes. The weekend breakfasts were the best. They kept us full to keep us from fighting. French toast was on Sundays, but they didn't use nutmeg (because you can get loaded on it), they didn't use many eggs, and the syrup was watery. Good French toast should taste like eggs and this stuff was subpar. Saturdays was grand slam: eggs, hash browns, bacon, pancakes. They wanted to keep everyone full so we'd just go back in our cells and relax. My first breakfast out of prison was candy I bought at a Greyhound bus depot and I ate it on the bus ride home. Later that night my first real sit-down meal was a plate of real French toast at Du-par's on Ventura Boulevard. It was 4 a.m. The French toast was eggy. The maple syrup was real. And it tasted like freedom.

Big-Batch Party Beans

Makes about
5 CUPS

When I was kid, rice and beans was a staple that we survived and thrived on. When I go to a restaurant and they ask, "Do you want rice and beans with that?" I'm like, "Well, yeah!?"

It's just a part of any meal. My grandma used to buy fifty-pound bags of dried pinto beans and our job as kids was to take the little rocks out of them. She'd boil the beans then smash 'em up and pan-fry them. Even my mom had beans simmering on the stove all day long. We ate beans not just with rice, but almost like a building block for other dishes too—we'd spread cheese over them and top 'em with pico de gallo. As the day went on, people ate down the beans and you'd thin the beans out with water and make a soup. This pot of beans has all the spirit and flavor of those long-simmered pots like Mom's, but without having to wait around all day for them, thanks to the convenience of canned beans.

¼ cup olive oil

1 white onion, minced

4 garlic cloves, smashed

1 (29-ounce) or 2 (15-ounce) cans black beans, drained and rinsed

¼ teaspoon kosher salt, plus more to taste

Freshly ground black pepper

1 bay leaf

1 dried chile de árbol

1 slice bacon, roughly chopped

1 cup chicken stock or water

In a large saucepan, heat the olive oil over medium-low heat. Add the onion and garlic and sauté until soft and translucent, about 10 minutes. Add the beans, salt, pepper to taste, bay leaf, chile, bacon, and chicken stock and stir to combine. Bring to a low boil, then reduce the temperature to a simmer and cook, stirring occasionally, until the beans are very soft, the ingredients are melded, and the mixture thickens some, about 30 minutes. Add ¼ cup of water at a time if the beans look dry at any point. Taste and adjust the seasoning, adding salt and pepper if needed.

Super Green Rice

Serves **4**

If you're a student of the Trejo culinary canon (translation: You already own a copy of the *Trejo's Tacos* cookbook), you know how to make Spanish rice, that yellow-pink rice served with combo platters at Mexican joints. So it's high time you learn to make a slightly healthier vibrantly green version that goes great with the Big-Batch Party Beans (opposite) and any of the proteins in this book.

2 tablespoons olive oil

½ medium white onion, minced

1 garlic clove, minced

1 cup jasmine rice

1 teaspoon kosher salt

½ small jalapeño, seeded and chopped

1 cup loosely packed fresh cilantro leaves, chopped

1 cup loosely packed spinach, chopped

In a medium saucepan, heat the oil over medium heat until shimmering, about 2 minutes. Add the onion, garlic, and rice and cook, stirring, until the rice is coated with oil and opaque, about 3 minutes.

In a blender, combine 2 cups water, the salt, jalapeño, cilantro, and spinach and blend until smooth. Add the mixture to the saucepan. Increase the heat to high to briefly bring the mixture to a boil. Reduce to a simmer, cover, and cook until tender and all the liquid is absorbed, about 15 minutes. Remove from heat and fluff with a spoon.

Big-Batch Party Beans

Mexican Slaw

Super Green Rice

Mexican Slaw

Makes about

4½ CUPS; SERVES 4 TO 6

A crunchy tangy coleslaw is a great way to balance the bold, smoky flavors of a Mexican feast. This slaw is full of good-for-you, fiber- and vitamin-packed red cabbage and tangy pickled red onions. Toasty pistachios add a nutty crunch.

¼ cup pistachios

½ to 1 jalapeño, finely chopped,

1 tablespoon grated lime zest

Juice of 2 limes, plus more to taste

2 tablespoons olive oil

1 teaspoon ground cumin

½ teaspoon ground coriander

½ teaspoon kosher salt, plus more to taste

Freshly ground black pepper

½ large head red cabbage, very thinly shredded

¼ cup Quick Pickled Red Onions (page 194)

1 cup loosely packed chopped cilantro

¼ cup crumbled Cotija cheese

Preheat the oven to 350°F.

Spread the pistachios out on a baking sheet and bake until lightly toasted and crunchy, about 10 minutes, taking care to not let them burn. Allow them to cool completely, then roughly chop.

In a large bowl, combine the jalapeño, lime zest, lime juice, olive oil, cumin, coriander, salt, and pepper to taste. Add the shredded cabbage, pickled onions, and cilantro and toss thoroughly to combine. Taste and add more salt or lime juice if needed. Garnish with the crumbled Cotija and chopped pistachios and serve.

Chai-Spiced Apple Empanadas

Makes about
12 EMPANADAS

Before you could get chicken and beef empanadas in LA, the only empanadas I ever had as a kid were sweet and filled with pumpkin, pineapple, or apple. These empanadas take the Indian chai spice mix that all the LA hipsters drink in their lattes to make one hell of a modern version of one of my favorite nostalgic childhood desserts.

Empanada Dough (recipe follows)

Filling

3 pounds Granny Smith apples (about 9)

2 tablespoons fresh lemon juice

¼ cup packed light brown sugar

2 tablespoons all-purpose flour

½ teaspoon kosher salt

½ teaspoon fennel seeds

½ teaspoon ground cinnamon

¼ teaspoon ground cloves

¼ teaspoon ground cardamom

2 tablespoons unsalted butter

Assembly

All-purpose flour, for rolling out

2 large eggs, separated and lightly beaten

Glaze

3 cups confectioners' sugar

5 tablespoons fresh Key lime or Persian lime juice

1½ teaspoons Lyle's Golden Syrup, light corn syrup, or honey

¾ teaspoon ground cinnamon

Make the empanada dough at least 30 minutes (and up to 24 hours) before making the empanadas.

MAKE THE FILLING: Peel, core, and dice the apples. In a large bowl, toss the apples with the lemon juice, brown sugar, flour, salt, fennel, cinnamon, cloves, and cardamom.

In a large skillet, melt the butter over medium heat. Add the apple mixture and cook, stirring occasionally, until the apples are cooked and tender but not totally falling apart, about 10 minutes. Let cool.

ASSEMBLE THE EMPANADAS: Shortly before you are ready to assemble the empanadas, remove one disk of dough from the refrigerator, lightly flour a work surface, and roll the dough into a roughly 12 × 18-inch sheet. Line two baking sheets with parchment paper.

Using a round mold, a small plate, or bowl about 5 inches in diameter, cut out dough rounds for filling. Gather and reroll the dough scraps to cut more rounds.

recipe continues

Place the rounds on one of the parchment-lined baking sheets and either refrigerate until ready to continue or assemble the empanadas immediately. Repeat the rolling, cutting, and refrigerating with the second disk of dough and the second prepared baking sheet.

Add about 2 tablespoons of filling to the center of each dough round, taking care not to overstuff it. Brush the edges of the empanada dough rounds with the egg whites. Fold the empanada rounds in half over the filling and seal the edges by pressing gently with your fingers. Use a fork to press the edges down to help fully seal the empanadas. Lightly brush the tops of the empanadas with the egg yolks. Transfer to the refrigerator for 30 minutes (or until ready to bake).

Preheat the oven to 400°F.

Bake one sheet of empanadas at a time, until the pastry is golden, 20 to 25 minutes. Transfer the cooked empanadas to a wire rack to cool.

MAKE THE GLAZE: Sift the confectioners' sugar into a large bowl. In a small bowl, combine the lime juice, golden syrup, and cinnamon. Add the liquid mixture to the confectioners' sugar and whisk together until smooth.

Using a rubber spatula, spread the glaze over the top of the empanadas. Let the glaze set up, about 5 minutes, before serving.

EMPANADA DOUGH

MAKES ENOUGH FOR ABOUT 12 EMPANADAS

3 cups all-purpose flour, plus more for dusting

½ teaspoon fine sea salt

1 stick (4 ounces) unsalted butter, very cold, cut into 1-inch cubes

1 large egg yolk

1 cup cold whole milk

In a food processor, pulse the flour and salt to combine. Add the butter and pulse until the texture resembles very coarse cornmeal. Don't overmix, as this will make the dough tough.

Add the egg yolk and gradually add the milk, ¼ cup at a time, pulsing until the dough starts to form clumps. The dough will not look totally combined at this point, and might even seem on the dry side.

Using your hands, gather the dough on a lightly floured surface and form it into 2 balls. Flatten the balls into disks, wrap them tightly in plastic wrap, and refrigerate for at least 30 minutes and up to 24 hours.

Cornmeal-Crusted Calamari and Shrimp
WITH HABAÑERO TARTAR SAUCE

Serves 4

My uncles and dad used to disappear for a day and come back with yellowtail and other fish they caught off the California coast. My mom would fry up their haul and we'd have a feast. This crispy calamari and shrimp fry reminds me of those meals.

1 cup gluten-free flour (we like King Arthur's Gluten Free Measure for Measure Flour)

1 cup fine cornmeal

½ teaspoon ground cumin

¼ teaspoon cayenne

½ teaspoon ancho chile powder

1 teaspoon dried oregano

1 teaspoon kosher salt, plus more to taste

1 teaspoon freshly ground black pepper

4 cups canola or safflower oil

12 jumbo shrimp, peeled and deveined

1 pound squid, cleaned and cut into ½-inch rings

Habanero Tartar Sauce (page 149)

Lime and lemon wedges, for squeezing

In a large bowl, combine the flour, cornmeal, cumin, cayenne, ancho powder, oregano, salt, and pepper and mix thoroughly with a fork or whisk.

In a large, deep pot, heat 2 inches of oil to 350°F over medium-high heat, about 7 minutes.

Set two small cooling racks over a baking sheet or line a baking sheet with paper towels.

Add the shrimp and squid to the bowl with the spiced cornmeal-flour mixture and toss to evenly coat. Using a spider strainer, carefully lower the shrimp and squid into the oil in batches, taking care not to let oil splash or crowd the pan. Cook the seafood for 1 minute, then gently stir to keep the shrimp and squid from sticking together. Continue to cook until each piece of seafood is golden brown and cooked through, 3 to 5 minutes longer.

Using the spider strainer, carefully remove the seafood, letting the excess oil drip back into the pot. Transfer to the racks or paper towels. Salt to taste and serve immediately with tartar sauce and lime and lemon wedges, for squeezing.

"Horchata" Smoothie

Makes
1 SMOOTHIE

This vegan smoothie is made with rice milk and has a creamy texture thanks to banana, chia seeds, and dates. It's packed with healthy fats and protein and is a great pre- or post-workout meal.

8 ounces (1 cup) unsweetened rice milk

1 tablespoon chia seeds

1 banana, broken into 3 or 4 chunks and frozen

1 tablespoon almond butter

1 pitted date, roughly chopped

¼ teaspoon ground cinnamon

⅛ teaspoon vanilla extract

4 ice cubes

In a blender, combine the rice milk and chia seeds and let sit for about 20 minutes until the chia seeds plump up and form a gel-like consistency.

Add the frozen banana, almond butter, date, cinnamon, vanilla, and ice. Blend until all of the ingredients are incorporated. Pour into a tall glass and serve immediately.

Cacao Chile Smoothie

Makes
1 SMOOTHIE

Whether for breakfast or for a post-workout boost, this vegan smoothie is sweet and savory and a solid foundation for healthy eating.

12 ounces (1½ cups) unsweetened vanilla almond milk

1 banana, broken into 3 or 4 chunks and frozen

1 pitted date, roughly chopped

1 tablespoon peanut butter

1 tablespoon unsweetened cacao powder

½ teaspoon ancho chile powder

4 ice cubes

In a blender, combine all of the ingredients and blend until smooth and frothy. Pour into a tall glass and serve immediately.

Mexican food might be the most delicious cuisine on the face of the planet. I can proudly stand by that. And you know what? It wasn't invented by a bunch of kings and rich people bossing around the kitchen staff at the castle. It was honest, hardworking moms and abuelas doing their best to feed their families food that was affordable. The meat is typically not expensive, but man, when they stew it right with all the spices it's better than prime rib. Tortillas are nutritious and you can wrap them around anything. And when they go stale, even better, you can fry them and turn them into chips. Nothing is wasted. Everything is tasty. A little goes a long way. And leftovers are what make the next day even easier and just as—if not more—delicious.

The recipes in this chapter can be snacks, meals, or scaled up in size to be party food. You could serve a big tray of taquitos for a party or fry a few and freeze the rest for quick weeknight meals. The recipes in this chapter are casual, come as you are, make it your own way kind of food. You're going to find master recipes for tostadas and empanadas and long-stewed beef that can either go in a taquito or be piled on a tostada. In Mexican cuisine, the stewing technique is known as a guisado: After all the chopping, just let the ingredients simmer and the flavors meld, and slow-cooking over time does the rest of the work. Make a big batch and use the guisado in a taco one day, on a tostada the next, or double it up and make it the day before a party (it actually often tastes better the next day).

The burger empanada filling (inspired by classic LA drive-through burgers, hence the pickles) can also make a cheeseburger-style taco if you put it in a tortilla and top it with shredded cheese. The chicken tinga can top a tostada, fill a taquito, or be happy in an empanada.

A lot of these dishes vibe on the LA street-food scene that ranks as one of the most diverse and exciting in the world. But it wasn't always like this. There was a period when the only food trucks out there were serving gringo food. I remember my buddies Johnny Martinez and Carlos Diaz had the idea to hire Mexican women to cook Mexican food on a truck—this was back in the early seventies. I'm not saying they invented it necessarily, but they were the first guys I knew who took a truck and served tacos from it. You could say I kind of followed in their footsteps.

Olvera Street–Style Chicken Taquitos

If you want to experience old-school Olvera Street culinary royalty, please patronize Cielito Lindo, a taquito stand that's been making this iconic dish since 1934. My dad and uncles used to take me there when I was a kid and I make a point of stopping by whenever I can. Crunchy on the outside, tender on the inside. Dip 'em in avocado salsa Cielito Lindo–style, and you're good to go. To make taquitos a healthier affair, we spritz them with cooking spray and bake them in the oven to cut back on the fat while preserving the crunch.

Poached Chicken

- 1 medium white onion, quartered
- 4 garlic cloves, peeled
- 2 celery stalks, halved crosswise
- 2 carrots, halved crosswise
- 1 bay leaf
- 2 pounds boneless, skinless chicken breast
- 1 teaspoon kosher salt

Filling

- 1 tablespoon vegetable oil
- 1 medium white onion, diced
- 2 garlic cloves, minced
- ¼ teaspoon ground cumin
- 1 teaspoon kosher salt
- 2 canned chipotle peppers in adobo sauce, chopped
- 1 (15-ounce) can tomato sauce

Taquitos

- Cooking spray
- 2 dozen corn tortillas
- Avocado Salsa (page 134)

POACH THE CHICKEN: In a stockpot, combine the onion, garlic, celery, carrots, bay leaf, chicken, salt, and 5 cups water. Bring to a boil, then reduce to a simmer and cook until the chicken is cooked through but tender, about 20 minutes. Remove the chicken and let it cool. Reserve 1 cup of the poaching liquid. Using two forks, shred the chicken into very small pieces.

MAKE THE FILLING: In a large skillet, heat the oil over medium heat until shimmering, about 3 minutes. Add the onion and garlic and cook, stirring occasionally, until soft, about 4 minutes. Add the cumin, salt, chipotles, tomato sauce, and shredded chicken. Reduce the heat to medium-low. Simmer, stirring occasionally, until slightly reduced and not too watery, 10 to 15 minutes. You want the sauce to be fairly tight so it won't make your taquitos soggy.

MAKE THE TAQUITOS: Preheat the oven to 400°F. Lightly mist two baking sheets with cooking spray.

Working in batches of 4, wrap a stack of tortillas in a wet paper towel and place on a plate. Microwave for 30 seconds to soften. Spoon ¼ cup filling down the center of each tortilla. Roll each tortilla tightly and place seam side down, ½ inch apart, on one of the prepared baking sheets. Lightly mist with cooking spray. Repeat with remaining tortillas.

Bake until light golden brown and crispy, about 15 minutes.

Serve with avocado salsa, for dipping.

Cantina Hack
TAQUITO DO-AHEAD

Taquitos are an amazing make-ahead party food. Simply cook up a batch the day before a party. Let them cool, place them in one layer on a lightly oiled baking sheet, cover the sheet in plastic wrap, and refrigerate. If you don't have a big enough refrigerator, store them in a resealable plastic bag. Reheat them on a pan in a 350°F oven.

Cantina Hack
ROLL YOUR OWN

I love a taquito any which way, and we've got you covered with other proteins that could be used as taquito fillings: Carne Deshebrada (page 187), Chicken Tinga (page 188), and the carnitas that top the Fight-Night Nachos Supreme (page 163) are all delicious rolled up in a taquito cooked according to the directions here. Or you could do as my grandma did and wrap a hot dog in a tortilla and then deep-fry it. It was like a Mexican pig in a blanket.

Pollo Asado
a la Brasa

Serves 4

Red-tinged chickens on the grill all juicy and smoky are a beautiful sight and enjoyed by just about every Latin American culture there is, from Argentina to Guatemala to LA. The Peruvians have their pollo a la brasa served with a super-spicy, garlicky ají sauce. We've combined the best of these worlds in this recipe. Round this out with beans and rice and you've got a killer dinner.

⅓ cup soy sauce

¼ cup fresh lime juice

¼ cup fresh orange juice

1 bunch of cilantro

5 garlic cloves, peeled

2 tablespoons ground cumin

1 teaspoon paprika

2 tablespoons achiote paste

½ teaspoon dried oregano

1 tablespoon vegetable oil

1 whole chicken (3½ pounds), cut into 2 breast quarters and 2 leg quarters

Lime wedges, for squeezing

Ají Sauce (page 139)

In a blender, combine the soy sauce, lime juice, orange juice, cilantro, garlic, cumin, paprika, achiote paste, oregano, and vegetable oil and blend until thoroughly combined, about 1 minute.

In a large bowl, combine the marinade and chicken. Cover the bowl with plastic wrap and marinate in the refrigerator for at least 4 hours or up to 12 hours.

About 30 minutes before cooking, remove the chicken from the refrigerator to allow it to come to room temperature.

Set up a charcoal or gas grill for two-zone cooking. If you're using charcoal, bank the coals higher on one half of the grill, leaving a single layer of coals on the other half. If you're using a gas grill, set one side to medium heat and the other side to low.

Arrange the chicken quarters across the hotter side of the grill, skin side down, and cook for 5 minutes. Turn the chicken and cook for another 5 minutes. Move the chicken to the cooler side of the grill if any fat flares up, to prevent the chicken from burning. Continue to cook, turn, and move the chicken as necessary until it's lightly browned and cooked through, and an instant-read thermometer reads 160°F in the thickest part of each piece.

Serve with lime wedges for squeezing and ají sauce on the side.

Carne Deshebrada

Makes about
4 CUPS

This is a perfect example of the brilliance of the guisado, or stewing, method. You take a humble and tough cut of beef like chuck, combine it with a few cheap and flavorful ingredients, and simmer it gently until the chuck gets all shreddy and tender and all the chiles and tomatoes combine into a simple and homey beefy cross-platform component that can keep for days in the fridge. Load it into tacos, roll up in a taquito, or use as a topping on a tostada. Add a crema, some salsa, cilantro, and chopped onions and serve it "con todo"-style. If you're going to use it in taquitos, which is what I recommend, be sure to shred the beef extra fine so you can roll the taquitos up tight.

- 2 pounds boneless beef chuck, cut into slabs 2 inches thick
- 2 teaspoons kosher salt, plus more to taste
- 2 medium white onions, finely diced
- 4 garlic cloves, minced
- 1 tablespoon vegetable oil
- 1 (28-ounce) can whole peeled tomatoes
- 3 serrano chiles, seeded and chopped
- 1 canned chipotle pepper in adobo sauce, chopped
- 2 tablespoons adobo sauce from the can of chipotles

In a large pot or Dutch oven, combine the chuck, salt, half of the onions, half the garlic, and 8 cups water. Bring to a simmer over medium heat and cook, partially covered, until the meat is tender, about 1½ hours.

Remove the cooked beef and set aside to let cool, reserving 1 cup of cooking liquid (discard the remainder). Once the meat is cool enough to handle, shred the beef into strands in a large bowl or on a cutting board, using your fingers or two forks.

In a large skillet, heat the oil over medium heat until shimmering, about 2 minutes. Add the remaining onions and garlic and cook, stirring occasionally, until soft and translucent, about 5 minutes.

Meanwhile, set a sieve over a bowl and pour in the canned tomatoes. Measure out and reserve ½ cup of the juices. Roughly chop the tomatoes.

Add the tomatoes, reserved tomato juice, serranos, chipotle pepper, adobo sauce, and reserved beef cooking liquid and cook until the tomatoes have broken down and the sauce has tightened up, 7 to 10 minutes. Add the shredded meat, stir, and simmer for 3 minutes. Taste and add salt if desired.

Chicken Tinga Tostadas

Makes
12 TOSTADAS

The tostada proves my theory of Mexican comfort food: It all comes down to how crunchy you want your tortilla. For a taco, most of the time you want it soft and you want to eat it fast: Heat up a tortilla, top it with meat and salsa and whatever, and you've got a fast and filling meal right there by the truck or the stand while it's tender. For a taquito, you're going to get your tortilla half crunchy and half soft in the oven, then dip it in salsa and nibble on it like you do with any party food. You can make a bunch ahead of time and put them out for guests—they won't fall apart. But for a tostada, it's all about showing off your ingredients, about big-time good looks, and big-time good crunch. You top a crispy flat fried tortilla with beautiful fillings and the freshest cilantro, crema, and pickled onions, and it's a texture sensation. A tostada is like a little circular work of art, especially when topped with chicken tinga, which is comfort food at its best. This is the kind of dish that, believe it or not, you can pull together in half an hour or so after doing a little chopping, opening a few cans, and simmering it all down.

Quick Pickled Red
  Onions (page 194)

Chicken Tinga

2 tablespoons
  vegetable oil

½ medium white
  onion, thinly sliced

2 garlic cloves,
  minced

1½ pounds boneless,
  skinless chicken
  thighs

1 (15-ounce) can
  tomato sauce

3 tablespoons
  chopped canned
  chipotle peppers
  in adobo sauce

Tostadas

12 (6-inch) tostada
  shells

Sour cream,
  for garnish

¼ cup chopped
  fresh cilantro

½ medium white
  onion, diced

At least 30 minutes before you plan to serve the tostadas, make the pickled onions.

MAKE THE CHICKEN TINGA: In a large skillet, heat the vegetable oil over medium heat until shimmering, about 3 minutes. Add the sliced onion and cook, stirring occasionally, until soft and translucent, about 4 minutes. Add the garlic and cook for another minute. Increase the heat to medium-high and add the chicken. Cook, without stirring, for about 3 minutes, to allow the chicken to develop a little color. You want it light brown. Add the tomato sauce and chipotles, reduce the heat to a simmer, cover and cook, stirring occasionally, until the meat is tender and shreddable, about 20 minutes. Remove from the

recipe continues

heat and use two forks to shred the chicken by pulling in opposite directions with the fork tines.

ASSEMBLE THE TOSTADAS: Top each tostada shell with ¼ cup chicken tinga, a dollop of sour cream, pickled onions, cilantro, and diced onion. Serve immediately for maximum crunch!

Cantina Hack
JACKFRUIT TINGA

This tinga is just as amazing when you make it vegan with jackfruit, the tropical superfood that gets all shreddy and delicious when you braise it slow and low. The first time I had it in our jackfruit tacos at the restaurant I coulda sworn it was carne asada. It's super easy to substitute jackfruit for chicken in this recipe. Get yourself 2 (20-ounce) cans of jackfruit in brine and drain the jackfruit. Add it when you would have added the chicken. You can skip the browning step. You'll need to increase the cooking time to around 45 minutes because it can take a while for the jackfruit to break down. Add a little water to the pan if it starts to dry out. You'll be blown away by how good it is!

Cantina Hack
DIY BAKED TOSTADA SHELLS

For a lighter alternative to store-bought fried tostadas, bake your own. Simply preheat the oven to 400°F. Arrange corn tortillas in a single layer on a baking sheet, mist them on both sides with cooking spray, and lightly sprinkle with salt. Bake for 5 minutes on one side. Flip the tortillas over, and bake until they're golden brown and crunchy, another 5 to 10 minutes. Easy, fast, and a great way to use leftover tortillas.

Tuna Tostadas
WITH CRISPY GARLIC

Makes
8 TOSTADAS

If I'm the O.G. of LA Mexican-ish food, then Nobu is the O.G. of popular Japanese-ish food. This tostada is a nod to the badass sushi chef who is probably talked about in more hip-hop songs than I am. He tops his new-style sashimi and other dishes with garlic, and this sushi-inspired tostada does the same. I like to think it represents the best of two great LA restaurant powerhouses.

¼ cup vegetable oil

5 large garlic cloves, sliced into chips

Kosher salt

12 ounces sashimi-grade tuna

¼ cup soy sauce

¼ cup fresh orange juice

1 tablespoon olive oil

Tostadas

8 (6-inch) tostada shells

3 tablespoons Chipotle Lime Crema (page 148)

1 avocado, sliced into 16 crescent-shaped pieces

¼ cup chopped fresh cilantro

Lime wedges, for squeezing

Line a small plate with paper towels. Heat a medium skillet over medium heat. Add the vegetable oil and heat until shimmering but not smoking, about 4 minutes. Add the garlic chips and fry them until light golden brown, taking care to not let them burn, stirring occasionally, about 4 minutes. Using a slotted spoon or tongs, remove the garlic from the oil and transfer to the paper towels to drain. Season to taste with kosher salt.

Slice the tuna into slices ⅓ inch thick, taking care to cut against the grain so the slices hold together. In a medium bowl, combine the soy sauce, orange juice, and olive oil and stir to thoroughly combine. Add the tuna slices and gently stir to coat them evenly with sauce.

ASSEMBLE THE TOSTADAS: Spread each tostada with some chipotle lime crema, and top with the tuna, avocado slices, garlic chips, and cilantro. Serve with lime wedges for squeezing.

Shrimp Tostadas with Avocado and Lime Crema

Tuna Tostadas with Crispy Garlic

Spicy Crab Tostadas

Shrimp Tostadas
WITH AVOCADO AND LIME CREMA

Makes
8 TOSTADAS

Seafood tostadas are a specialty in coastal Mexico, particularly in Ensenada, where surfers and foodies make pilgrimages to eat fresh-caught shrimp topped with all kinds of bright and spicy toppings. These shrimp tostadas get topped with quick mashed avocados and a rich, spicy-tangy lime crema. It makes a great and light date-night meal. Or prepare this with the other seafood tostadas—Tuna Tostadas with Crispy Garlic (page 191) and Spicy Crab Tostadas (page 195)—and throw a Baja-inspired "beach" party in your backyard.

Avocado Mash

2 avocados, halved and pitted

Juice of ½ lime

½ teaspoon kosher salt

Shrimp Topping

1 tablespoon unsalted butter

1 pound jumbo shrimp (about 16 total), peeled and deveined

Tostadas

8 (6-inch) tostada shells

Chipotle Lime Crema (page 148)

Quick Pickled Red Onions (recipe follows)

¼ cup chopped fresh cilantro

8 lime wedges, for squeezing

MAKE THE AVOCADO MASH: Scoop the avocado flesh into a medium bowl. Add the lime juice and salt and mash with a fork until nearly smooth. You don't want it too chunky because you want to be able to spread it on a tostada. Set aside.

PREPARE THE SHRIMP: In a large skillet, melt the butter over medium heat, about 2 minutes. Add the shrimp and cook until they are pink and no longer translucent on one side, about 4 minutes. Turn the shrimp over and cook the other side until they are pink and no longer translucent throughout, about 4 minutes longer. Transfer the shrimp to a cutting board. When cool enough to handle, cut into ½-inch pieces.

ASSEMBLE THE TOSTADAS: Using the back of a spoon, spread about 3 tablespoons avocado mash on each tostada all the way to the edge. Top with about ¼ cup chopped shrimp. Spoon chipotle crema over everything, top with pickled onions and cilantro, and serve with lime wedges on the side.

recipe continues

QUICK PICKLED RED ONIONS

MAKES 2 CUPS

1 medium red onion, halved and thinly sliced

1 teaspoon kosher salt

¾ cup apple cider vinegar

Place the sliced red onions in a glass jar and sprinkle with the salt. Add the vinegar, close the lid tightly, and shake the jar. Refrigerate for at least 30 minutes. The onions will absorb the vinegar and salt, soften, and turn a beautiful shade of pink.

Spicy Crab Tostadas

Makes
8 TOSTADAS

Sweet lump crabmeat sauced with mayo, lime juice, and two kinds of chile makes this spicy crab tostada rich, punchy, and refreshing all at the same time.

1 cup lump crabmeat (from an 8-ounce container; check for shells)

1 tablespoon plus 1 teaspoon fresh lime juice, plus more to taste

⅓ cup mayonnaise

1 teaspoon minced fresh jalapeño, plus more to taste

½ teaspoon minced fresh habanero, plus more to taste

½ teaspoon kosher salt, plus more to taste

Tostadas

8 (6-inch) tostada shells

1 cup thinly shredded red cabbage

1 avocado, sliced into 16 crescent-shaped pieces

¼ cup finely chopped fresh cilantro

In a bowl, combine the crabmeat, lime juice, mayonnaise, jalapeño, habanero, and salt and stir to combine. Taste, adding more lime juice, salt, or chiles as desired.

ASSEMBLE THE TOSTADAS: Top each tostada with a layer of shredded cabbage. Dividing evenly, spoon the crab mixture on the tostadas. Garnish with avocado slices and cilantro.

Danger Dogs

Makes

6 DANGER DOGS

On weekends in neighborhoods with lots of bars, near USC or Dodger Stadium on game nights, or outside the Hollywood Bowl, you'll sometimes see shopping carts with sheet pans wired to the top and burners underneath like a makeshift griddle. The street cart cooks will be sizzling jalapeños, onion, peppers, and hot dogs wrapped in, yes, bacon! In Los Angeles we call them Danger Dogs, streetside Dodger Dogs, Sonoran Hot Dogs, or Tijuana Dogs. Whatever you call them, they're insanely delicious and great for a party. Make the caramelized onion-pepper mix in advance and put out a bunch of toppings for a party.

Onions and Peppers

2 tablespoons vegetable oil

1 small medium onion, thinly sliced

½ medium red bell pepper, thinly sliced

½ medium green bell pepper, thinly sliced

Kosher salt

2 jalapeños, quartered lengthwise

Danger Dogs

6 hot dogs

6 slices bacon

2 tablespoons vegetable oil

Ketchup

Mayonnaise

Mustard

6 hot dog buns

COOK THE ONIONS AND PEPPERS: In a large skillet, heat the oil over medium heat for about 1 minute. Add the onion and cook, stirring occasionally, until lightly caramelized, 5 to 7 minutes. Add the red and green peppers and cook, stirring occasionally, until the peppers are soft and caramelized, about 10 minutes. Remove the onion-pepper mixture from the skillet, season to taste with kosher salt, and set aside.

Add the jalapeños to the skillet, skin side down, and cook over medium heat, without moving, for 5 minutes, until a char develops on the skin. Turn them over and cook for another 5 minutes or so, until tender. Set aside. Keep the skillet for the hot dogs.

MAKE THE DANGER DOGS: Tightly wrap the hot dogs in bacon from end to end. Add the oil to the skillet, return the heat to medium, and heat the pan until the oil is shimmering, about 2 minutes. Add the hot dogs and cook until browned, about 5 minutes. Give the hot dogs a quarter turn and cook for another 5 minutes. Repeat two more times until the bacon is crisped on all sides. (Alternatively, if you're making lots of hot dogs for a crowd, preheat the oven to 400°F. Place the bacon-wrapped dogs on a foil-lined baking sheet, and cook until the bacon is crisped, 20 to 30 minutes.)

Spread ketchup, mayonnaise, and mustard on each bun, top with some onion-pepper mixture, a jalapeño slice, then place a bacon-wrapped hot dog on top and serve immediately.

recipe continues

Cantina Hack

DIY DANGER DOG TOPPING BAR

In addition to the usual ketchup, mayo, and mustard, go full bore and blow your guests away with a killer selection of a few or all the topping options below.

* **Pico de Gallo (page 152)**

* **Chipotle Lime Crema (page 148)**

* **Diced avocado**

* **Pickled jalapeño**

* **Mexican Thousand Island Dressing (page 140)**

* **Crunchy Salsa Macha (page 145)**

* **Canned pinto beans, drained and rinsed**

* **Sour cream**

Street Tacos al Pastor

Serves **8**

It's hard to imagine, but there was a time when taco trucks didn't even exist in LA. There were food trucks that sold sandwiches and breakfast to construction crews, but nothing like today, with every imaginable region of Mexico represented, from Sinaloa to Michoacán, and trucks specializing in birria and al pastor. Al pastor is maybe the most dramatic of taco offerings, with its big spinning "trompa" or stacked marinated pork sizzling on a vertical rotisserie with a piece of pineapple on top. The taqueros slice it off and chop it up and sizzle on the griddle and serve it with chunks of pineapple, radishes, and avocado salsa. Here we get the same deliciously flavorful charred taco truck effect, no trompa required.

8 dried guajillo chiles, seeded

2 dried chiles de árbol, seeded

1 pineapple, peeled and cored

½ medium yellow onion, diced

1 jalapeño, seeded and diced

8 garlic cloves, peeled

1 cup distilled white vinegar

¼ cup sugar

2 tablespoons achiote paste

½ teaspoon ground cumin

½ teaspoon dried oregano

1 tablespoon kosher salt

3 pounds boneless pork shoulder, sliced into steaks ½ inch to ¾ inch thick

Tacos

2 dozen corn tortillas, warmed

½ medium yellow onion, diced

1 cup chopped fresh cilantro

Avocado Salsa (page 134)

Badass Blender Salsa (page 151)

6 medium red radishes, thinly sliced

In a medium saucepan, bring 2 cups water to a boil over medium-high heat. Add both dried chiles and cook for 1 minute, then remove from the heat. Let the chiles sit in the hot water until soft, about 20 minutes.

Cube half of the pineapple and cut the other half into rings ½ inch thick.

In a blender, combine the chiles, chile soaking liquid, cubed pineapple, onion, jalapeño, garlic, vinegar, sugar, achiote paste, cumin, oregano, and salt. Blend the mixture until smooth, 1 to 2 minutes.

In a large resealable heavy-duty freezer bag, combine the pork steaks and the marinade and refrigerate for at least 12 hours and up to 24 hours.

recipe continues

Set up a charcoal or gas grill for two-zone cooking. If you're using charcoal, bank the coals higher on one half of the grill, leaving a single layer of coals on the other half. If you're using a gas grill, set one side to medium heat and the other side to low.

Grill the pineapple slices over the hotter side until grill marks appear, about 3 minutes. Turn the pineapple slices over and cook the other side, about 3 minutes more. Dice the grilled pineapple and set aside.

Using tongs, remove the pork from the marinade, allowing any excess liquid to drip back into the bag. Grill the pork on the hotter side of the grill, turning occasionally, until it's caramelized, lightly charred, and cooked through, about 15 minutes total. If the pork begins to burn or char too quickly, transfer it to the cooler side as needed. Transfer the cooked pork to a platter and let rest for 10 minutes to let the juices settle. If you slice it too soon, the flavorful juices will run out onto the cutting board. Slice thinly.

ASSEMBLE THE TACOS: Serve the pork slices on warm corn tortillas and garnish with diced grilled pineapple, diced onion, cilantro, both salsas, and radish slices.

Burger Empanadas

Makes about
12 EMPANADAS

When I was a kid, the only empanadas we had were sweet—filled with pineapple, apple, and pumpkin—and I couldn't get enough of them. Today we serve savory beef empanadas at Trejo's Cantina catering events. In these, chopped dill pickles give the beef empanadas the flavors of a classic LA hamburger. That said, you should feel free to stuff the empanadas with whatever you want—like Chicken Tinga (page 188) or Carne Deshebrada (page 187).

**Empanada Dough
(page 172)**

Filling

**2 tablespoons
olive oil**

**1 medium onion,
diced**

**3 garlic cloves,
minced**

1 pound ground beef

**2 teaspoons ancho
chile powder**

**2 teaspoons ground
cumin**

**1 teaspoon chipotle
chile powder**

**2 teaspoons dried
oregano**

**1 teaspoon
kosher salt**

**½ teaspoon
freshly ground
black pepper**

**¼ cup canned
crushed tomatoes**

**1 (4-ounce) can diced
Hatch chiles**

**⅓ cup diced
dill pickles**

⅓ cup pickle juice

Assembly and Serving

**All-purpose flour,
for rolling**

**2 large eggs,
separated and
lightly beaten**

**Green Dipping Sauce
(page 138), for
serving**

Make the empanada dough at least 30 minutes (and up to 24 hours) before preparing the empanadas.

MAKE THE FILLING: In a large skillet, heat the oil over medium heat. Add the onion and garlic and sauté until softened, about 5 minutes. Add the ground beef, ancho powder, cumin, chipotle powder, oregano, salt, and black pepper. Cook until the beef is no longer pink, about 8 minutes.

Add the tomatoes, Hatch chiles, pickles, and pickle juice. Reduce the heat to medium-low and simmer, stirring occasionally, until the juices thicken, about 15 minutes. Taste and adjust the seasoning.

If not making the empanadas immediately, cool and store the filling in an airtight container in the refrigerator for up to 2 days. Bring to room temperature before using.

ASSEMBLE THE EMPANADAS: Shortly before you are ready to assemble the empanadas, remove one disk of dough from the refrigerator, lightly flour a work surface, and roll the dough into a roughly 12 × 18-inch sheet. Using a round mold, a small plate, or bowl approximately 5 inches across as a guide, cut out dough rounds for filling. Gather the scraps and reroll to cut more rounds.

Place the rounds on a parchment-lined baking sheet and either refrigerate until ready to continue or assemble the empanadas immediately. Repeat the rolling, cutting, and refrigerating with the second disk of dough and a second baking sheet.

Add about 2 tablespoons of filling to the center of each dough round, taking care not to overstuff them. Brush the edges of the empanada dough rounds with the egg whites. Fold the empanada rounds in half over the filling and seal the edges by pressing gently with your fingers. Use a fork to press the edges down to help fully seal the empanadas. Lightly brush the top of the empanadas with the egg yolks. Transfer to the refrigerator to rest for 30 minutes (or until ready to bake).

Preheat the oven to 400°F.

Bake one sheet of empanadas at a time until the pastry is golden, 20 to 25 minutes. Transfer the empanadas to a wire rack to cool.

Serve warm with a side of the dipping sauce.

Cantina Hack
FILLING SWAPS

Like so many preparations in this book, empanadas are a blank canvas waiting for your artistry. If you're going to make empanadas filled with Chicken Tinga (page 188) or Tijuana–Style Beef Birria (page 209), make sure to drain some of the sauce from these meats so the empanadas don't get soggy. Other fillings that work: the carnitas from the Fight–Night Nachos Supreme (page 163), the chicken filling from Olvera Street–Style Chicken Taquitos (page 182), Carne Deshebrada (page 187), or Jackfruit Tinga (page 190).

Arrachera Steak

Serves **4 TO 6**

How could I not be a sucker for a Brazilian churrascaria? You know what I'm talking about: those palaces of paleo perfection where waiters with skewers of stacked beef take swords and slice them onto your plate until you cry uncle from being so stuffed. This simple skirt steak takes the best of Argentina (meat and garlicky chimichurri sauce) and Mexico (a limey, chile-spiked, cumin-y marinade). Use this to anchor a backyard barbecue on a hot summer day.

2 tablespoons Worcestershire sauce

1 tablespoon soy sauce

1 tablespoon chopped canned chipotle peppers in adobo sauce

4 garlic cloves, minced

2 teaspoons ground cumin

2 teaspoons dried oregano

Juice of 2 limes

Juice of 1 orange

2 pounds skirt steak

Roasted Jalapeño Chimichurri (page 135)

Corn tortillas, warmed, for serving

In a large bowl, combine the Worcestershire sauce, soy sauce, chipotles, garlic, cumin, oregano, lime juice, and orange juice. Add the skirt steak, making sure the marinade covers as much as possible. Marinate for at least 2 hours or up to 12 hours, turning the steak over halfway through.

Heat a grill, large skillet, or grill pan to medium-high. Remove the steak from the marinade, let the marinade drip back into bowl, and pat the steak dry. Place the steak on the grill grates or in the pan and let cook, without moving, until browned, 4 to 6 minutes. Turn the steak over and cook to medium-rare or medium, another 4 minutes or so. Remove from the heat and let it rest for 10 minutes to allow the juices to settle. Once the steak has rested, place it on a cutting board and cut against the grain into ¼-inch-thick slices.

Serve with the chimichurri on the side and warm corn tortillas.

Tijuana-Style Beef Birria

Serves **8**

In recent years, people in LA have gone nuts for Tijuana-style beef birria. It's another one of those "guisado" or stewed preparations that turns an affordable cut of meat into a tender taco topping. What's even cooler is that they serve it with a little cup of the red chile-tinged cooking liquid on the side. We make our version with some beef short ribs for extra richness and the additional flavor you get when you cook with bones.

Tomato-Chile Sauce

2 ancho chiles, seeded

6 dried guajillo chiles, seeded

1½ teaspoons tamari or soy sauce

1 (28-ounce) can crushed tomatoes

½ cup distilled white vinegar

6 medium garlic cloves, peeled

2 teaspoons dried oregano

1 teaspoon dried thyme

1 teaspoon ground cumin

½ teaspoon ground cinnamon

¼ teaspoon ground ginger

Birria

3 pounds beef chuck, cut into 4-inch chunks

2 pounds bone-in short ribs

1½ tablespoons kosher salt

¼ cup canola oil

1 cup finely diced white onion

1 teaspoon ground cinnamon

4 whole cloves

2 bay leaves

1 teaspoon freshly ground black pepper

For Serving

24 corn tortillas, warmed

½ cup chopped fresh cilantro

½ cup finely diced white onion

2 limes, quartered

MAKE THE TOMATO-CHILE SAUCE: In a large dry skillet, toast the dried chiles over medium-high heat for 30 to 45 seconds on one side until fragrant. Turn the chiles over and toast them for 30 to 45 seconds more. Remove from the heat.

In a medium pot, bring 2 cups water to a boil. Remove the pot from heat, add the toasted chiles, and let them soften for about 20 minutes.

In a blender, combine the chiles and their soaking liquid, the tamari or soy sauce, tomatoes, vinegar, garlic, oregano, thyme, cumin, cinnamon, and ginger and blend until smooth.

MAKE THE BIRRIA: Preheat the oven to 350°F.

Season both of the meats on all sides with the salt. In a large ovenproof pot, such as a Dutch oven, heat the oil over high heat until smoking, 3 to 4 minutes. Working in batches so you don't crowd the pan, add the meat and don't move it until it's developed a nice brown sear, about 5 minutes. Turn the meat and let sear for another 5 minutes. Repeat until all sides are browned. Transfer the meat to a large plate or tray.

recipe continues

Reduce the heat to medium, add the onion, and cook, stirring occasionally, until soft and golden, about 5 minutes. Return the meat to the pot and add the tomato-chile sauce. Add enough water to cover the meat—4 to 6 cups depending on the size of your pot. Add the cinnamon, cloves, bay leaves, and black pepper.

Cover, transfer to the oven, and bake until the meat is tender, about 2 hours. The meat should shred easily. If it doesn't, continue to cook, checking every 15 minutes, until it shreds. Skim any excess fat off the top and reserve for quesabirrias (see Cantina Hack, right). Using a slotted spoon, transfer the meat to a large bowl and shred using two forks. Reserve the cooking liquid for serving.

Serve the beef on warm corn tortillas, topped with cilantro and onion, with lime wedges on the side for squeezing. Serve with small bowls of the reserved cooking liquid for sipping.

Cantina Hack
QUICK QUESABIRRIA

If you're lucky enough to have leftover birria the next day, cook it up in a quesadilla, aka a quesabirria. Pour a few tablespoons of the reserved cooking fat into a large skillet over medium heat. Place a corn tortilla in the pan, top with Mexican cheese blend and birria, and fold the tortilla over when it's soft. Cook a few minutes on each side and serve with cooking liquid on the side.

Chorizo Smash Burgers

WITH MEXICAN THOUSAND ISLAND DRESSING

Makes

4 BURGERS

Before places like Shake Shack and Smashburger started pressing their beef into super-thin patties and making it "a trend," the only kind of burgers were smash burgers. That's what you always got at a diner, every drive-through, and eventually the legendary California burger chain In-N-Out. In my smash burger, beef is mixed with spicy chorizo to make it super savory, and Mexican Thousand Island dressing gives it a spicy herby kick.

1 pound ground beef

½ pound fresh chorizo, removed from casings

4 slices Monterey Jack cheese

4 hamburger buns

¼ cup Mexican Thousand Island Dressing (page 140)

1 large tomato, cut into ¼-inch-thick slices

1 medium white onion, cut into ¼-inch-thick slices

1 avocado, cut into ¼-inch-thick slices

In a large bowl, combine the beef and chorizo and mix with your hands until thoroughly combined. Form 4 patties, each ½ inch thick.

Heat a large heavy-bottomed skillet over medium heat, about 5 minutes. Place the patties in the pan, smashing down with a large spatula to ensure that the meat is in full contact with the hot pan and to slightly flatten the patty further. Work in batches, if necessary, so as not to crowd the pan. Cook the patties, without moving, until well browned, about 5 minutes. The fat should be rendering and the edges of the patties pulling away from the pan slightly. Turn each patty over and place a slice of Monterey Jack on the cooked side. Cook until the cheese is melted and the meat is cooked through, 3 to 5 minutes longer.

Meanwhile, lightly toast the buns.

Spread both sides of each bun with the Thousand Island dressing. Add a patty to each bun and top with some of the tomato, onion, and avocado. Serve immediately.

Super-Easy Tamales

Makes
30 TAMALES

If you've never made tamales because you think they're difficult, this recipe will change your mind. With just an hour of prep, you'll have two dozen fluffy, amazing tamales to eat for dinner, lunch the next day, with leftovers to freeze and eat down the road. This recipe uses the classic cheese and chile filling, but you can use any fillings in this book, like Chicken Tinga (page 188), or the Beef Birria (page 209), or Jackfruit Tinga (page 190).

30 dried corn husks

1½ cups olive oil

10 cups (2 pounds) masa harina, such as King Arthur

1 teaspoon baking powder

1½ teaspoons kosher salt

3½ cups vegetable or chicken broth

2 (8-ounce) packages shredded Mexican cheese blend

2 (10-ounce) cans roasted chiles, such as Hatch, roughly chopped

Soak the corn husks in a large bowl filled with water until soft, about 1 hour. Place a few cans of beans on top to keep them submerged.

In another large bowl, combine the olive oil, masa harina, baking powder, salt, and broth. Mix with your hands until a pliable dough forms. Knead until smooth, 3 to 5 minutes.

Place a corn husk on a cutting board with the wide end toward you. Using a large spoon, spread ¼ cup of dough in the center. Shape it into a rough round about 4 inches in diameter. Place 2 tablespoons of cheese lengthwise in the center of the dough. Sprinkle 1 tablespoon of chiles on top of the cheese.

Lift the two sides of the corn husk in toward the center like a book so the two sides of masa meet and cover the filling, then, holding the excess corn husk together, fold and wrap it to one side around the tamale. Fold the top and bottom ends over the tamale and turn it over to hold the folded sides down. Repeat until you have about 30 tamales.

In a large pot fitted with a steamer basket, add enough water to just come up to the level of the steamer basket. Working in batches, arrange the tamales vertically in the steamer basket and turn the heat to medium. Once the water starts to steam, cover the basket and cook until the tamales are fluffy and tender and the cheese is melted, from 30 minutes to 1 hour, depending on how many you cook at a time. The tamales are super tender when they come out of the basket, but will firm up as they sit. Let them cool for 30 minutes before serving. You can also let the tamales completely cool and freeze for up to 1 month.

NOTE:
To freeze the tamales to enjoy at a later date, allow the cooked tamales to cool completely and then freeze them in an airtight container or plastic freezer bags for up to 1 month. When ready to use, let them thaw in the fridge, and then reheat them in the steamer basket.

Cornmeal Waffles
WITH ANCHO-MEZCAL MAPLE SYRUP

Makes about
SIX 4-INCH WAFFLES OR THREE 6-INCH WAFFLES

I've probably been to more diners than most Angelenos, from the Original Pantry downtown, where I'd go for late-night meals with my old pal Eddie Bunker on our midnight walks, to Du-par's at the original Farmer's Market, where Eddie and I'd always order a stack of pancakes to split between the two of us in addition to our eggs and hash browns and whatever else we were having. If we really wanted to go for it, we'd get an order of waffles, a next-level indulgence because they just call out for maple syrup and whipped cream and all sorts of toppings to get into those crevices. These waffles are punched up with cornmeal and served with a spicy-smoky mezcal and chile maple syrup. If you don't drink alcohol, simply leave out the mezcal and the syrup will still be delicious thanks to the butter and that hit of chile heat.

Ancho-Mezcal Maple Syrup

1 cup maple syrup

3 tablespoons mezcal

2 tablespoons butter

¼ teaspoon ancho chile powder

1 teaspoon smoked paprika

¼ teaspoon cayenne pepper

Waffles

¾ cup cornmeal

¾ cup gluten-free flour

1 tablespoon sugar

¼ teaspoon baking soda

¼ teaspoon baking powder

¼ teaspoon kosher salt

¼ teaspoon ground cinnamon

1¼ cups buttermilk

2 large eggs

2 tablespoons butter, melted

For Serving

Whipped cream

10 strawberries, hulled and quartered

2 bananas, cut into ½-inch-thick slices

MAKE THE ANCHO-MEZCAL MAPLE SYRUP: In a medium saucepan, combine the maple syrup, mezcal, and butter and bring to a boil over medium-high heat. Reduce to a simmer, add the ancho powder, smoked paprika, and cayenne and stir to combine. Remove the syrup from the heat and let it sit until ready to serve.

MAKE THE WAFFLES: In a large bowl, whisk together the cornmeal, gluten-free flour, sugar, baking soda, baking powder, salt, and cinnamon. In a medium bowl, whisk together the buttermilk, eggs, and melted butter. Pour the buttermilk mixture into the cornmeal mixture and whisk until smooth. Let the mixture sit for 10 minutes so it rises a bit.

Preheat the oven to 250°F.

recipe continues

Preheat your waffle iron. Cook the waffles in batches according to the manufacturer's directions. Transfer cooked waffles to a baking sheet and keep warm in the oven.

TO SERVE: Top the waffles with whipped cream, strawberries, bananas, and mezcal syrup and serve immediately.

Cantina Hack
WAFFLES FOR DINNER

If you're not wanting all that sugar or feel like having waffles for dinner, make a savory version and top the waffles with fried eggs, sliced avocado, and crumbled bacon, and sprinkle it with Tajín. Or to make our version of chicken and waffles, pick up a copy of the Trejo's Tacos cookbook for our fried chicken recipe and you'll be tapping into that Southern food trend that made its way to LA.

TREJO'S RECIPES
for Success

Just like each recipe in this book is a little list of instructions where you start with a pile of ingredients and end up with something delicious, inspiring quotes have been a key ingredient in my fifty-plus years of success at turning my life around and being of service to the people. They're short, sweet, and get me through tough times. Here are the quotes and sayings that you could say are my recipes for success.

"Education is the key to anything you want to do."

Whenever I talk at grade schools and high schools I make this critical point to all the kids and teenagers. The more you learn, the more options you have, plain and simple. Back in my day, especially in the Latin community, people thought about high school as being the end. My dad graduated from high school and went straight to work in construction. As a result, I didn't even think about college or a trade, both of which open up a world of opportunities. Whether

you want to be an electrician or a lawyer, you've got to get the right education and get educated so you can do your trade at the highest level.

"It's better to shoot for the moon and miss than aim for the gutter and make it."

I still remember the day I thought of that one. It was when I was at San Quentin, and I was walking around the track with my buddy Tyrone, another inmate. He and I were shooting the shit and he asked me what my life goals were and I said "Man, I want to be both the lightweight and welterweight boxing champion of San Quentin." And Tyrone said "Man, you're aiming pretty low." But that was my world and it was hard for me to see beyond it. But the thing is, you can change your world, no matter how hard or stuck it feels. And listening to another inmate without getting defensive, which was huge for me, broke me out of that shortsighted view. I came up with that phrase in the penitentiary, but still remember it and repeat it when I'm faced with a challenge and need to rise to the occasion. I shot for the moon, got out of prison, and stayed out. But I'm proud to say before that happened I still became the lightweight and welterweight boxing champion of San Quentin.

"Everything good that's ever happened to me has been a direct result of helping someone else."

I've shared this quote with kids in schools, hardened inmates in prisons, guys trying to kick drugs and alcohol, to my family and friends when they're having a hard time, and to myself every day. Help someone. Every day. And you will help yourself. And it doesn't have to be big. My first day out of prison I took the trash out for my elderly neighbor and it made me feel just good enough to not go out and get loaded. And I kept at that for fifty-plus years. It can be as little as saying good morning to a stranger. You'll feel better. Period. For some folks it's the hardest thing in the world to do. It was for me when I got out of the pen, where I'd been trained to be icy cold and intimidating just to survive. So you gotta train yourself to do the opposite. It's as basic as saying to yourself: I'm going to say

good morning to the first stranger I meet every day. If you've got kids, give them your time. Have lunch with your kids. Compliment them. Give them self-esteem. A little boost every day. Every morning I wake up and say a prayer that I sign every autograph and take every picture with every fan I see. People are happy. I'm happy. And then it catches and you find yourself helping people all the time and you'll be surprised by how much good stuff comes back to you.

"I might as well be myself because everyone else is taken."

This one helps when you're down on yourself or you see somebody and you wish your life was like theirs and say to yourself: I want to be that person. Nope, you can't. That person is taken. Don't judge your inside by someone else's outside. You're you and you have to work with what you have, play into your good side, face the stuff that you need to change. Only by working on being the better you are you going to have a good life. And it's going to be yours and yours alone.

"The light at the end of the tunnel isn't a train."

When someone is down and having a hard time I say this because: a) the future is never as bad as folks think it is and when you move ahead and face it you learn you can get through it and grow despite what you imagined it would be. And b) it's just funny and laughter is the key. If you can laugh a little it relaxes you and helps you see your way out of a problem. And when you really think about it, there is no such thing as the future. The future is right now.

ACKNOWLEDGMENTS

I would like to thank my Trejo's Tacos partners, Ash Shah and Jeff Georgino, for their constant commitment and support, both professionally and personally. I especially want to mention some truly incredible members of the Trejo's Tacos team: Hugo Escobedo, Karla Duffy, and Jim Busfield. In the midst of the uncertainty and chaos of 2020, you rolled up your sleeves and worked tirelessly at the restaurants and then with me in the community—at great sacrifice to yourselves and your families—to feed the frontline heroes; the homeless and most vulnerable among us; and anyone else who just needed the comfort a fresh hot meal can provide. It is because of your heart, sweat, and commitment to our mission that the grills at Trejo's Tacos were able to stay warm and keep bellies full. I am very proud of and grateful to you and to all of the Trejo's Tacos crew and family.

A big thank-you to the bookmakers: Hugh Garvey, Ed Anderson, Lillian Kang, the immensely talented Kim Stodel for crafting some insanely delicious cocktails and nonalcoholic drinks, and Aimee Garvey; and the entire team at Clarkson Potter, including Raquel Pelzel, Bianca Cruz, Jen Wang, Mark McCauslin, Kelli Tokos, Merri Ann Morrell, Kristin Casemore, and Stephanie Davis.

Additional thanks to Madam Tussauds, El Cholo, Northgate Gonzalez Market, and Musso and Frank for opening your doors to us.

A huge amount of appreciation goes to the M's in my life—Mariette Matekel, Mario Castillo, Michael Castillo, and Max Martínez—and also Carlos Díaz and Ali Carbajal. My life is made easier because of you. Thank you for all you do.

And to my fans, you are a constant source of motivation and never have you lifted me up more than during the last couple of years. I am humbled by your love and inspired by your passion. Thank you for your support!

I also give special thanks to Johnny Harris, who has been my mentor and sponsor since 1963. And to all of the others who have helped me on this journey, too many to mention here; but you know who you are.

To my dear friend and agent of almost thirty years, Gloria Hinojosa, and the entire team at Amsel, Eisenstadt, Frazier & Hinojosa. Thank you for steering the ship called my career and for your guidance, direction, and friendship. You always have my back and have influenced my life in so many ways. I love you dearly, GS.

Finally, to my family: without you there is no me. You are my world and the air that I breathe. Everything is for you.

INDEX

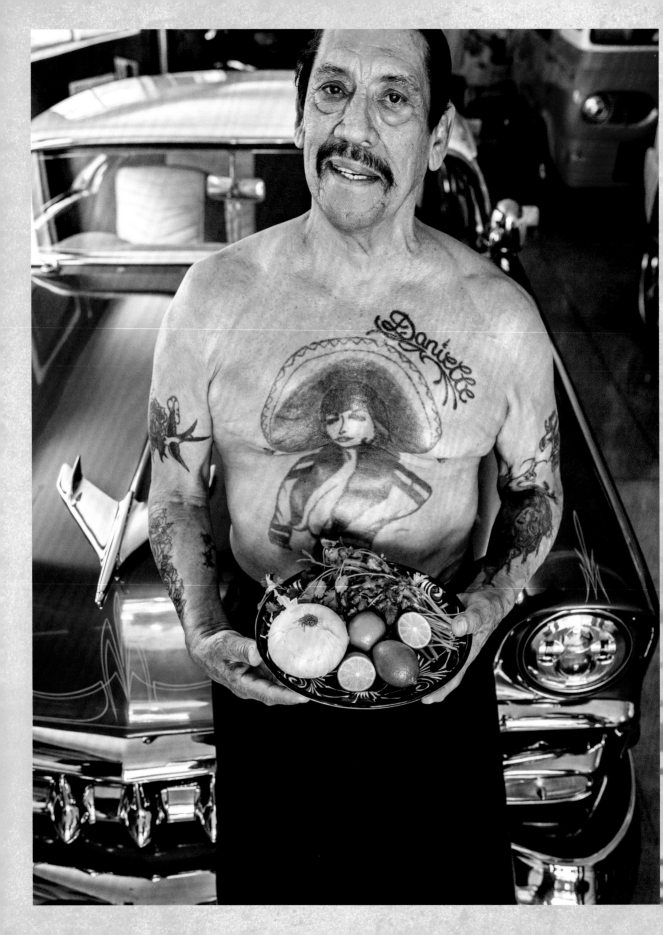